THE
UNKNOWN
Where No One Has Been

Troll Target Series

Troll

TROLL TARGET SERIES

Lewis Gardner	*Senior Editor*
Miriam Rinn	*Editor*
Meish Goldish	*Teaching Guide*
Elizabeth A. Ryan	*Bibliographies*
Peter Pluchino	*Cover Illustration*

PROJECT CONSULTANT

David Dillon   *Professor of Language Arts,*
                      McGill University, Montreal

ACKNOWLEDGEMENTS

"The Strange Valley" by T.V. Olsen was first published in *Great Ghost Stories of the Old West* (Four Winds, 1968) edited by Betty Baker. Copyright © 1968 by T.V. Olsen. Published by arrangement with Golden West Literary Agency. All rights reserved.

"Childhood" reprinted from Maura Stanton: *Cries of Swimmers*. By permission of Carnegie Mellon University Press. Copyright © 1984 by Maura Stanton.

(Acknowledgements continued on page 159)

Printed in the United States of America.   ISBN 0-8167-4737-7

10 9 8 7 6 5 4 3 2 1

Contents

The Strange Valley

by T. V. Olsen

When beings get together ... which ones are the ghosts?
It's not easy to understand what you're seeing—when
it's something you've never seen before.

The three horsemen came up on the brow of a hill, and the valley was below them. It was a broad cup filled by the brooding thickness of the prairie night. The light shed by a narrow sickle of moon picked out just another Dakota valley, about a mile across as the white men reckoned distance, and surrounded by a rim of treeless hills. The valley floor was covered by an ordinary growth of a few small oaks, a lot of brush, and some sandy flats with a sparse lacing of buffalo grass.

Young Elk said, "Is this what you wish us to see, Blue Goose?" He made no effort to keep the skepticism from his voice.

"Yes," said the rider on his left. "This is the place."

"Now that we're here, tell us again what you saw the other night." The third youth, the shaman's son, sounded very intent. "From where did it come?"

"From there." Blue Goose leaned forward as he pointed toward the eastern end of the valley. "As I told you, I'd had a long day of hunting, and I was very tired. I made my camp in the center of the valley, and fell asleep at once. This was about sunset.

"It was long after dark when I woke. I came awake all at once, and I don't know why. I heard a strange sound, a kind of growl that was very low and steady, and it was a long way off. But it was running very fast in my direction, and I sat in my blanket and waited."

Young Elk said with a grim smile, "Because you were too afraid even to run."

Blue Goose was silent for a moment. "Yes," he said honestly. "I was afraid. I didn't know what the thing was, but I knew it was getting closer. And growling louder all the while, as if in great pain or anger. Then I saw it.

"It was a huge beast, as big as a small hill, black in the night and running very close to the ground, and its two eyes were yellow and glaring. It went past me very close, but so fast I didn't think it saw me. It was bellowing as loud as a hundred bull buffaloes if they all bellowed at once. Suddenly it was gone."

"What do you mean, it was gone?" Young Elk demanded. "You said that before."

"I'm not sure. All I know is that suddenly I saw it no more and heard it no more."

"I wish you could tell us more about it," said the shaman's son. "But I suppose it was very dark."

"Yes," Blue Goose agreed. "Even a little darker than tonight." He hesitated. "I thought that the thing might be covered with scales— bright scales like a huge fish—since the moon seemed to glint on it here and there. But I couldn't be sure."

"You're not very sure of anything," Young Elk gibed.

Blue Goose sighed. "I do not know what I saw. As I have said, I left the valley very fast and camped a long way off that night. But I came back in the morning. I looked for the thing's spoor. I looked all over, and there was nothing. Yet I found where I had camped, and my pony's tracks and my own. But the thing left no sign at all."

"Because there had never been a thing. You should be more careful about what you eat, my friend." Young Elk spoke very soberly, though he felt like laughing out loud. "Spoiled meat in one's belly is like *mui waken,* the strong drink. It has a bad effect on the head."

For a little while the three young Sioux sat their ponies in silence, looking down into the dark stillness of the valley. A silky wind pressed

6

up from the valley floor, a wind warm with the summer night and full of the ripening smells of late summer.

But something in it held a faint chill, and that was strange. Young Elk felt a crawl of gooseflesh on his bare shoulders, and he thought: *The night is turning cold, that is all.* He felt the nervous tremor run through his mount.

He laid his hand on the pony's shoulder and spoke quietly to the animal. He was angry at Blue Goose, his best friend, for telling this foolish story and angry at himself for coming along tonight with the other two because he was deeply curious. And back in their camp only a few miles to the north there was firelight and laughter and a warm-eyed girl named Morning Teal, and Young Elk was a fool to be out here with his friend and with the son of that tired old faker of a medicine man.

Of late, Young Elk thought sourly, there had been more than the usual quota of wild stories of visions and bad spirits running rampant among the people. Early this same summer, on the river of the Greasy Grass that the whites called Little Big Horn, the long-haired General Custer had gone down to defeat and death with his troops. Many warriors of their own band had been among the twelve thousand Sioux, Cheyenne, and Arapaho who had helped in the annihilation of a hated enemy.

In the uneasy weeks since, as the people followed the buffalo, hunting and drying meat in the prospect of being driven back to the reservation by white cavalry, a rash of weird happenings were reported. Men who had died were seen walking the prairie with bloody arrows protruding from them. Voices of the dead were heard in the night wind. It was the shaman's part to encourage this sort of nonsense. A man claimed that a bluecoat soldier he had scalped appeared to him nightly with the blood still fresh on his head. The shaman chanted gibberish and told him to bury the scalp so that the ghost would trouble his nights no more.

Young Elk was disgusted. He had never seen even one of these spirits. Only the fools who believed in such things ever saw them.

The shaman's son broke the long pause, speaking quietly. "This valley is a strange place. Today I spoke with my father and told him what Blue Goose has told us. He said that he knows of this place, and that his father's fathers knew of it too. Many strange things happened here in the old days. Men known to be long dead would be seen walking—not as spirits, but in the flesh. Still other things were seen, things too strange to be spoken of. Finally all our people of the Lakotas came to shun the valley. But that was so long ago that even most of the old ones have forgotten the stories."

Young Elk made a rude chuckling sound with his tongue and teeth.

"Young Elk does not believe in such things," the shaman's son observed. "Why then did he come with us tonight?"

"Because otherwise for the next moon I would hear nothing from you and Blue Goose but mad stories about what you saw tonight. I'd prefer to see it for myself."

"Oh," said Blue Goose, "then there *was* something? I did not make this great story out of the air?"

"Maybe not." Young Elk said slyly, "Maybe it was the white man's iron horse that Blue Goose saw."

"Now you jest with me. Even though I am not all-wise like Young Elk, still I know that the iron horse of the *wasicun* runs on two shining rails, and there are no rails here. And the iron horse does not growl thus, nor does it have two eyes that flame in the dark."

Another silence stretched among the three youths as they sat their ponies on the crest of the hill and peered down into the dark valley. And Young Elk thought angrily, *What is this?* They had come here to go down in the valley and wait in the night, in hopes that the thing Blue Goose had seen would make another appearance. Yet they all continued to sit here as though a winter of the spirit had descended and frozen them all to the spot.

Young Elk gave a rough laugh. "Come on!" He kneed his pony forward, down the long grassy dip of hill. The others followed.

Near the bottom, Young Elk's pony turned suddenly skittish, and he had to fight the shying animal to bring him under control. Blue Goose and the shaman's son were having trouble with their mounts too.

"This is a bad omen," panted the shaman's son. "Maybe we had better go back."

"No," Young Elk said angrily, for his pony's behavior and the strange feeling of the place were putting an edge on his temper. "We've come this far, and now we'll see what there is to see, if anything. Where was Blue Goose when he thought he saw the beast?"

Blue Goose said, "We must go this way," and forced his horse through a heavy tangle of chokecherry brush. He led the way very quickly, as though afraid that his nerve would not hold much longer.

They came to a rather open stretch of sand flats that caught a pale glimmer of moonglow; it was studded with clumps of thicket and a few scrub oaks. "Here is the place," Blue Goose told them.

The three Sioux settled down to wait. Nobody suggested that it would be more comfortable to dismount. Somehow it seemed better to remain on their ponies and accept a cramp or two. It was only, Young Elk told himself, that they should be ready for anything, and they might have a sudden need of the ponies.

Once more it was the shaman's son who ended an interval of silence. "What time of the night did it happen, Blue Goose?"

"I can't be sure. But close to this time, I think."

Silence again. The ponies shuffled nervously. The wind hushed through some dead brush, which rattled like dry, hollow bird bones. Idly Young Elk slipped his throwing-ax from his belt and toyed with it. He slid his hand over the familiar shape of the flint head and the fresh thongs of green rawhide that lashed it to the new handle he had put on only this morning. His palm felt moist.

And his head felt slightly dizzy. Now the shapes of rocks, the black masses of brush, seemed to shimmer and swim; the landscape seemed misty and unreal as if seen through a veil of fog, yet there was no fog. *It is a trick of the moon,* Young Elk thought. He gripped the ax tighter; his knuckles began to ache.

"There!" Blue Goose whispered. "Do you hear it?"

Young Elk snapped, "I hear the wind," but even as the words formed on his lips the sound was increasing, unmistakably not the wind. Not even a gale wind roaring through the treetops of a great forest made such a noise. As yet he could see nothing, but he knew that the sound was moving in their direction.

Suddenly the two yellow eyes of which Blue Goose had spoken came boring out of the night. Now he could see the hulking black shape of the monster running toward them at an incredible speed and so low to the ground that its legs could not be seen. All the while the strange humming roar it made was steadily growing.

The ponies were plunging and rearing with fear. The shaman's son

9

gave a cry of pure panic and achieved enough control over his mount to kick it into a run. In a moment Blue Goose bolted after him.

Young Elk fought his terrified pony down and held the trembling animal steady, his own fear swallowed in an eagerness to have a closer look at the thing. But he was not prepared for the fury of its rush as it bore down toward him. And its round, glaring eyes blinded him—he could see nothing beyond them.

It let out a piercing, horrible shriek as it neared him—it was hardly the length of three ponies away—and it seemed to hesitate. It hissed at him, a long gushing hiss, while the yellow eyes bathed him in their wicked glare.

Young Elk waited no longer. He lunged his pony in an angling run that carried him past the thing's blunt snout, and in that moment brought his arm back and flung the ax with all his strength. He heard it make a strange hollow boom, although he did not see it hit, and then he was racing on through the brush, straining low to his pony's withers, heedless of the tearing branches.

Young Elk did not slow down till he reached the end of the valley; then he looked back without stopping. There was no sign of the beast. The valley was deserted and quiet under the dim moonlight.

Young Elk crossed the rim of hills and caught up with his friends on the prairie beyond. "Did you see it?" the shaman's son demanded eagerly.

"No. Its eyes blinded me. But I hit it with my ax." Young Elk paused; his heart was pounding so fiercely in his chest he was afraid they would hear it, so he went quickly on, "I heard the ax hit the thing. So it was not a ghost."

"How do you know?" countered the shaman's son. "Where did it go? Did you see?"

"No," Young Elk said bitterly. "It was very fast."

"Let's go back to camp," Blue Goose said. "I don't care what the thing was. I do not want to think about it."

Joe Kercheval had been dozing in his seat when his partner, Johnny Antelope, hit the brakes of the big truck and gave Joe a bad jolt. And then Joe nearly blew his stack when Johnny told him the reason he had slammed to an abrupt stop on this long, lonely highway in the middle of nowhere.

"I tell you, I saw him," Johnny insisted as he started up again and drove on. "A real old-time Sioux buck on a spotted pony. He was sitting on his nag right in the middle of the road, and I almost didn't stop in time. Then he came charging past the cab, and I saw him fling something—I think it was an ax—at the truck. I heard it hit. You were waking up just then—you must have heard it."

"I heard a rock thrown up by the wheels hit somewheres against the trailer, that's all," Joe said flatly. "You been on the road too long, kid. You ought to lay off a few weeks, spend a little time with your relatives on the reservation."

Johnny Antelope shook his head. "I saw him, Joe. And then I didn't see him. I mean—I could swear he disappeared—simply vanished into thin air—just as he rode past the cab. Of course it was pretty dark . . ."

"Come off it. For a college-educated Indian, you get some pretty far-out notions. I've made this run a hundred times and I never seen any wild redskins with axes, spooks or for real."

"You white men don't know it all, Joe. You're Johnny-come-latelies. This has been our country for a long, long time, and I could tell you some things . . ." Johnny paused, squinting through the windshield at the racing ribbon of highway unfolding in the tunneling brightness of the headlights. "I was just remembering. This is a stretch of land the Sioux have always shunned. There are all kinds of legends concerning it. I remember one story in particular my old granddaddy used to tell us kids—I guess he told it a hundred times or more . . ."

"Nuts on your granddaddy."

Johnny Antelope smiled. "Maybe you're right, at that. Old Blue Goose always did have quite an imagination."

"So does his grandson." Joe Kercheval cracked his knuckles. "There's a turnoff just up ahead, kid. Swing around there."

"What for, Joe?"

"We're going back to where you seen that wild man on a horse. I'm gonna prove to you all you seen was moonshine." Joe paused, then added wryly, "Seems like I got to prove it to myself, too. I say it was just a rock that hit the truck, and I'll be losin' sleep if I don't find out for sure."

Without another word Johnny swung the big truck around and headed back east on the highway. The two truckers were silent until Johnny slowed and brought the truck to a shrieking stop. The air brakes were still hissing as he leaned from the window, pointing. "Here's the spot, Joe. I recognize that twisted oak on the right."

"Okay, let's have a close look." They climbed out of the cab, and Johnny pointed out the exact spot where he had first seen the Indian warrior, and where the warrior had cut off the highway alongside the cab and thrown his ax.

"Look here, kid." Joe played his flashlight beam over the roadside. "Soft shoulders. If your boy left the concrete right here, his horse would of tromped some mighty deep prints in the ground. Not a sign, see?"

"Wait a minute," Johnny Antelope said. "Flash that torch over here, Joe." He stooped and picked up something from the sandy shoulder.

The halo of light touched the thing Johnny held in his outstretched hand. "Know what this is, Joe?" he asked softly. "A Sioux throwing-ax."

Joe swallowed He started to snort, "Nuts. So it's an ax . . ." but the words died on his lips.

For under the flashlight beam, even as the two men watched, the wooden handle of the ax was dissolving into rotted punk, and the leather fastenings were turning cracked and brittle, crumbling away. Only the stone blade remained in Johnny's hand, as old and flinty and weathered as if it had lain there by the road for an untold number of years. . . .

Childhood

by Maura Stanton

I used to lie on my back, imagining
A reverse house on the ceiling of my house
Where I could walk around in empty rooms
All by myself. There was no furniture
Up there, only a glass globe in the floor,
And knee-high barriers at every door.
The low silled windows opened on blue air.
Nothing hung in the closet; even the kitchen
Seemed immaculate, a place for thought.
I liked to walk across the swirling plaster
Into the parts of the house I couldn't see.
The hum from the other house, now my ceiling,
Reached me only faintly. I'd look up
To find my brothers watching old cartoons,
Or my mother vacuuming the ugly carpet.
I'd stare amazed at unmade beds, the clutter,
Shoes, half-dressed dolls, the telephone,
Then return dizzily to my perfect floorplan
Where I never spoke or listened to anyone.

I must have turned down the wrong hall,
Or opened a door that locked shut behind me,
For I live on the ceiling now, not the floor.
This is my house, room after empty room.
How do I ever get back to the real house
Where my sisters spill milk, my father calls,
And I am at the table, eating cereal?
I fill my white rooms with furniture,
Hang curtains over the piercing blue outside.
I lie on my back. I strive to look down.
The ceiling is higher than it used to be,
The floor so far away I can't determine
Which room I'm in, which year, which life.

The Third Level

by Jack Finney

Everyone dreams sometimes about escaping. If we found a way to get to a better world, would we take it? Charley would, if he could just find the right track ...

The presidents of the New York Central and the New York, New Haven and Hartford railroads will swear on a stack of timetables that there are only two. But I say there are three because I've been on the third level at Grand Central Station. Yes, I've taken the obvious step: I talked to a psychiatrist friend of mine, among others. I told him about the third level at Grand Central Station, and he said it was a waking-dream wish fulfillment. He said I was unhappy. That made my wish kind of mad, but he explained that he meant the modern world is full of insecurity, fear, war, worry, and all the rest of it, and that I just want to escape. Well, hell, who doesn't? Everybody I know wants to escape, but they don't wander down into any third level at Grand Central Station.

But that's the reason, he said, and my friends all agreed. Everything points to it, they claimed. My stamp-collecting, for example—that's a

14

"temporary refuge from reality." Well, maybe, but my grandfather didn't need any refuge from reality; things were pretty nice and peaceful in his day, from all I hear, and he started my collection. It's a nice collection, too, blocks of four of practically every U.S. issue, first-day covers, and so on. President Roosevelt collected stamps, too, you know.

Anyway, here's what happened at Grand Central. One night last summer I worked late at the office. I was in a hurry to get uptown to my apartment, so I decided to subway from Grand Central because it's faster than the bus.

Now, I don't know why this should have happened to me. I'm just an ordinary guy named Charley, thirty-one years old, and I was wearing a tan gabardine suit and a straw hat with a fancy band—I passed a dozen men who looked just like me. And I wasn't trying to escape from anything; I just wanted to get home to Louisa, my wife.

I turned into Grand Central from Vanderbilt Avenue and went down the steps to the first level, where you take trains like the Twentieth Century. Then I walked down another flight to the second level, where the suburban trains leave from, ducked into an arched doorway heading for the subway—and got lost. That's easy to do. I've been in and out of Grand Central hundreds of times, but I'm always bumping into new doorways and stairs and corridors. Once I got into a tunnel about a mile long and came out in the lobby of the Roosevelt Hotel. Another time I came up in an office building on Forty-sixth Street, three blocks away.

Sometimes I think Grand Central is growing like a tree, pushing out new corridors and staircases like roots. There's probably a long tunnel that nobody knows about feeling its way under the city right now, on its way to Times Square, and maybe another to Central Park. And maybe—because for so many people through the years Grand Central *has* been an exit, a way of escape—maybe that's how the tunnel I got into . . . but I never told my psychiatrist friend about that idea.

The corridor I was in began angling left and slanting downward and I thought that was wrong, but I kept on walking. All I could hear was the empty sound of my own footsteps and I didn't pass a soul. Then I heard that sort of hollow roar ahead that means open space, and people talking. The tunnel turned sharp left; I went down a short flight of stairs and came out on the third level at Grand Central Station. For just a moment I thought I was back on the second level, but I saw the room was smaller, there were fewer ticket windows and train gates, and the information booth in the center was wood and old-looking. And the man in the booth wore a green eyeshade and long, black sleeve-protectors. The lights were dim and sort of flickering. Then I saw why; they were open-flame gaslights.

There were brass spittoons on the floor, and across the station a glint of light caught my eye; a man was pulling a gold watch from his vest pocket. He snapped open the cover, glanced at his watch, and frowned. He wore a dirty hat, a black four-button suit with tiny lapels, and he had a big, black, handle-bar mustache. Then I looked around and saw that everyone in the station was dressed like 1890-something; I never saw so many beards, sideburns and fancy mustaches in my life. A woman walked in through the train gate; she wore a dress with leg-of-mutton sleeves and skirts to the top of her high-buttoned shoes. Back of her, out on the tracks, I caught a glimpse of a locomotive, a very small Currier & Ives locomotive with a funnel-shaped stack. And then I knew.

To make sure, I walked over to a newsboy and glanced at the stack of papers at his feet. It was the *World*; and the *World* hasn't been published for years. The lead story said something about President Cleveland. I've found that front page since, in the Public Library files, and it was printed June 11, 1894.

I turned toward the ticket windows knowing that here—on the third level at Grand Central—I could buy tickets that would take Louisa and me anywhere in the United States we wanted to go. In the year 1894. And I wanted two tickets to Galesburg, Illinois.

Have you ever been there? It's a wonderful town still, with big old frame houses, huge lawns, and tremendous trees whose branches meet overhead and roof the streets. And in 1894, summer evenings were twice as long, and people sat out on their lawns, the men smoking cigars and talking quietly, the women waving palm-leaf fans, with the fireflies all around, in a peaceful world. To be back there with the first World War still twenty years off, and World War II over forty years in the future . . . I wanted two tickets for that.

The clerk figured the fare—he glanced at my fancy hatband, but he figured the fare—and I had enough for two coach tickets, one way.

But when I counted out the money and looked up, the clerk was staring at me. He nodded at the bills. "That ain't money, mister," he said, "and if you're trying to skin me you won't get very far," and he glanced at the cash drawer beside him. Of course the money was old-style bills, half again as big as the money we use nowadays, and different-looking. I turned away and got out fast. There's nothing nice about jail, even in 1894.

And that was that. I left the same way I came, I suppose. Next day, during lunch hour, I drew $300 out of the bank, nearly all we had, and bought old-style currency (that *really* worried my psychiatrist friend). You can buy old money at almost any coin dealer's, but you have to pay a premium. My $300 bought less than $200 in old-style bills, but I didn't care; eggs were thirteen cents a dozen in 1894.

But I've never again found the corridor that leads to the third level at Grand Central Station, although I've tried often enough.

Louisa was pretty worried when I told her all this and didn't want me to look for the third level any more, and after a while I stopped; I went back to my stamps. But now we're *both* looking, every weekend, because now we have proof that the third level is still there. My friend Sam Weiner disappeared! Nobody knew where, but I sort of suspected because Sam's a city boy, and I used to tell him about Galesburg—I went to school there—and he always said he liked the sound of the place. And that's where he is, all right. In 1894.

Because one night, fussing with my stamp collection, I found— Well, do you know what a first-day cover is? When a new stamp is issued, stamp collectors buy some and use them to mail envelopes to themselves on the very first day of sale; and the postmark proves the date. The envelope is called a first-day cover. They're never opened; you just put blank paper in the envelope.

That night, among my oldest first-day covers, I found one that shouldn't have been there. But there it was. It was there because someone had mailed it to my grandfather at his home in Galesburg; that's what the address on the envelope said. And it had been there since July 18, 1894—the postmark showed that—yet I didn't remember it at all. The stamp was a six-cent, dull brown, with a picture of President Garfield. Naturally, when the envelope came to Granddad in the mail, it went right into his collection and stayed there—till I took it out and opened it.

The paper inside wasn't blank. It read:

> 941 Willard Street
> Galesburg Illinois
> July 18, 1894

Charley:

I got to wishing that you were right. Then I got to believing you were right. And, Charley, it's true; I found the third level! I've been here two weeks, and right now, down the street at the Dalys', someone is playing a piano, and they're all out on the front porch singing *Seeing Nellie Home*. And I'm invited over for lemonade. Come on back, Charley and Louisa. Keep looking till you find the third level! It's worth it, believe me!

The note is signed *Sam*.

At the stamp and coin store I go to, I found out that Sam bought $800 worth of old-style currency. That ought to set him up in a nice little hay, feed, and grain business; he always said that's what he really wished he could do, and he certainly can't go back to his old business. Not in Galesburg, Illinois, in 1894. His old business? Why, Sam was my psychiatrist.

Johanna

by Jane Yolen

Nightmares—and horror stories—often take place in dark, lonely forests. Johanna needs to cross the forest, but terrible things, she knows, can happen there.

The forest was dark and the snow-covered path was merely an impression left on Johanna's moccasined feet.

If she had not come this way countless daylit times, Johanna would never have known where to go. But Hartwood was familiar to her, even in the unfamiliar night. She had often picnicked in the cool, shady copses and grubbed around the tall oak trees. In a hard winter like this one, a family could subsist for days on acorn stew.

Still, this was the first night she had ever been out in the forest, though she had lived by it all her life. It was tradition—no, more than that—that members of the Chevril family did not venture into the midnight forest. "Never, never go to the woods at night," her mother said, and it was not a warning as much as a command. "Your father went though he was told not to. He never returned."

And Johanna had obeyed. Her father's disappearance was still in her memory, though she remembered nothing else of him. He was not the first of the Chevrils to go that way. There had been a great-uncle and two girl cousins who had likewise "never returned." At least, that was what Johanna had been told. Whether they had disappeared into the maw of the city that lurked over several mountains to the west, or into the hungry jaws of a wolf or bear, was never made clear. But Johanna, being an obedient girl, always came into the house with the setting sun.

For sixteen years she had listened to that warning. But tonight, with her mother pale and sightless, breathing brokenly in the bed they shared, Johanna had no choice. The doctor, who lived on the other side of the wood, must be fetched. He lived in the cluster of houses that rimmed the far side of Hartwood, a cluster that was known as the "Village," though it was really much too small for such a name. The five houses of the Chevril family that clung together, now empty except for Johanna and her mother, were not called a village though they squatted on as much land.

Usually the doctor himself came through the forest to visit the Chevrils. Once a year he made the trip. Even when the grandparents and uncles and cousins had been alive, the village doctor came only once a year. He was gruff with them and called them "Strong as beasts," and went away never even offering a tonic. They needed none. They were healthy.

But the long, cruel winter had sapped Johanna's mother's strength. She lay for days silent, eyes cloudy and unfocused, barely taking in the acorn gruel that Johanna spooned for her. And at last Johanna had said: "I will fetch the doctor."

Her mother had grunted "no" each day, until this evening. When Johanna mentioned the doctor again, there had been no answering voice. Without her mother's no, Johanna made up her own mind. She *would* go.

If she did not get through the woods and back with the doctor before dawn, she felt it would be too late. Deep inside she knew she should have left before, even when her mother did not want her to go. And so she ran as quickly as she dared, following the small, twisting path through Hartwood by feel.

At first Johanna's guilt and the unfamiliar night were a burden, making her feel heavier than usual. But as she continued running, the crisp night air seemed to clear her head. She felt unnaturally alert, as if she had suddenly begun to discover new senses.

The wind molded her short dark hair to her head. For the first time she felt graceful and light, almost beautiful. Her feet beat a steady tattoo on the snow as she ran, and she felt neither cold nor winded. Her steps lengthened as she went.

Suddenly a broken branch across the path tangled in her legs. She went down heavily on all fours, her breath caught in her throat. As she got to her feet, she searched the darkness ahead. Were there other branches waiting?

Even as she stared, the forest seemed to grow brighter. The light from the full moon must be finding its way into the heart of the woods. It was a comforting thought.

She ran faster now, confident of her steps. The trees seemed to rush by. There would be plenty of time.

She came at last to the place where the woods stopped, and cautiously she ranged along the last trees, careful not to be silhouetted against the sky. Then she halted.

She could hear nothing moving, could see nothing that threatened. When she was sure, she edged out onto the short meadow that ran in a downward curve to the back of the village.

Once more she stopped. This time she turned her head to the left and right. She could smell the musk of the farm animals on the wind, blowing faintly up to her. The moon beat down upon her head and, for a moment, seemed to ride on her broad, dark shoulder.

Slowly she paced down the hill toward the line of houses that stood like teeth in a jagged row. Light streamed out of the rear windows, making threatening little earthbound moons on the graying snow.

She hesitated.

A dog barked. Then a second began, only to end his call in a whine.

A voice cried out from the house furthest on the right, a woman's voice, soft and soothing. "Be quiet, Boy."

The dog was silenced.

She dared a few more slow steps toward the village, but her fear seemed to proceed her. As if catching its scent, the first dog barked lustily again.

"Boy! Down!" It was a man this time, shattering the night with authority.

21

She recognized it at once. It was the doctor's voice. She edged toward its sound. Shivering with relief and dread, she came to the backyard of the house on the right and waited. In her nervousness, she moved one foot restlessly, pawing the snow down to the dead grass. She wondered if her father, her great-uncle, her cousins had felt this fear under the burning eye of the moon.

The doctor, short and too stout for his age, came out of the back door, buttoning his breeches with one hand. In the other he carried a gun. He peered out into the darkness.

"Who's there?"

She stepped forward into the yard, into the puddle of light. She tried to speak her name, but she suddenly could not recall it. She tried to tell why she had come, but nothing passed her closed throat. She shook her head to clear the fear away.

The dog barked again, excited, furious.

"My God," the doctor said, "it's a deer."

She spun around and looked behind her, following his line of sight. There was nothing there.

"That's enough meat to last the rest of this cruel winter," he said. He raised the gun, and fired.

My Psychiatrist Tells Me I Have "Sci-Fitis"... But He Is One of Them!

by Bruce Watson

Bruce Watson wants us to believe that a strange invasion has taken place. Science-fiction movies have taken over his mind!

On an ordinary April day the weirdness came to town. Mine is a small, pleasant town, much like one you'd see in the movies. Nothing ever happens here. But one day some students at our elementary school went home with headaches. Our boys and girls were usually so healthy. What had gotten into them? Then teachers began to cough and wheeze. When the principal broke out in hives, the local health authorities closed the school to investigate. "No big deal," a team of experts said. "Just a fungus in the carpets. Pretty common these days." Everyone was satisfied, except me.

I grew up on B-movie science fiction. Raised on classics like *The Creature From Planet Zork* and *The Beast with 1,000 Toes,* I knew that truth was often stranger than science fiction. This fungus plot seemed familiar. Hadn't I seen the same scenario in *It Came From Beyond the Sun,* the movie in which a fungus from a distant asteroid chokes a small, pleasant town? What was going on here?

As our authorities debated how to kill it, the fungus grew out of the school carpet and up the walls. I knew there was only one solution. First we'd need a Professor with a white lab coat. Then we'd find the Town Blonde and an Average Guy With Heroic Shoulders. At a critical moment, we'd have the Professor turn to the Hero and say, "I'm afraid there's nothing that ordinary science can do, Steve. This thing's a monster!" Cue Steve, who slams his fist on the table. The Blonde screams. Then the Army rolls in tanks and blasts the fungus to smithereens. THE END.

But movies were not reality . . . not yet. In real life we got some federal cleanup money and scoured the school. The fungus was gone. Everyone was relieved, except me. I knew that once life began imitating B-movies, it was just . . . *The Beginning of the End* (the 1957 classic in which giant locusts eat Chicago, then cast a hungry eye on Milwaukee).

Soon my daughter started uttering "Heh heh, cool, heh heh!" She was normally such an articulate child. Then right next door, 7-year-old Jason turned on MTV and began gyrating around the room. Soon, children all over our pleasant town were thrashing to music, "talking trash," behaving like fiends. The P.T.A. blamed it on cable TV, but I knew we were living in . . . *The Village of the Damned* (the 1960 masterpiece in which aliens possess a town's children and make their eyes glow).

I couldn't remember how that damned village saved its children so I went to the P.T.A. meeting and said, "I'm afraid there's nothing that ordinary science can do, Steve. This thing's a monster!" Sadly, only a few parents agreed with my plan to blow the kids to smithereens. Some limited their kids to 40 hours of TV a week, but the rest watched helplessly as pleasant children turned into garbage-mouths.

Next the newspapers declared that it was no longer safe to eat anything! According to scientists, all our food—butter, margarine, meat, eggs, sugar, apples—contained chemicals! Some blamed the media for fear mongering, but I knew we were living in *Attack of the Giant Experts* (aliens plant electrodes in scientists' necks to control a small Midwestern town). In the sequel, *The Giant Experts Go to Washington,* the aliens brainwash Congress by implanting American-flag lapel pins in Congressmen's coats. The nation is saved when they herd all scientists and politicians into the Grand Canyon and call in the Army. THE END.

Blowing up experts may have worked in the 1950s, but these days there would be environmental concerns and lawsuits from lawyers named Steve. We were defenseless, bombarded by the latest studies and government reports!

What was happening? I turned to my wife and said, "You've got to believe me! The fungus, the fiendish kids, the evil experts . . . *I've seen all this before!*" She sent me to a psychiatrist who said I had *sci-fitis*, the delusion that life imitates B-movies. "But it's all true!" I said. "Don't you read the papers?" I whipped out the evening paper. All over the country, UFOs were abducting law-abiding citizens, just like in *Invaders from Mars.* Supermarkets were selling genetically grown veggies (*Attack of the Killer Tomatoes*). Millions were watching brain-killing TV shows and reading cat books (*Invasion of the Mind Snatchers*). "We've got to do something!" I told the shrink. Then I saw the electrodes in his neck.

The next morning I awoke, showered and went to the mirror. My God! Was that me? Once so young and striking. I had become . . . *The Incredible Aging Man* (the thriller in which a man looks more like his father every day). Then I checked the calendar. It was *1995!* Whenever an old sci-fi movie took place in the future, somewhere in the last reel Steve turned to the Professor and said, "But Professor Dreen! Surely you have a weapon that can keep the Monster from devouring Elm City! After all, it's 1995!" And now it was!

Every day I tell my daughter to turn off the TV. I tell my wife to skip the warnings, to eat anything she wants. I tell people our politicians are possessed. No one believes me. I'm afraid there's nothing that ordinary science can do. I slam my fist on the table. In the distance a blonde screams. Has anyone tried calling in the Army? THE END. Or is it just . . . the beginning?

Frankenstein

by Edward Field

The monster has escaped from the dungeon
where he was kept by the Baron,
who made him with knobs sticking out from each side of his neck
where the head was attached to the body
and stitching all over
where parts of cadavers were sewed together.

He is pursued by the ignorant villagers,
who think he is evil and dangerous because he is ugly
and makes ugly noises.
They wave firebrands at him and cudgels and rakes,
but he escapes and comes to the thatched cottage
of an old blind man playing on the violin Mendelssohn's
    "Spring Song."

Hearing him approach, the blind man welcomes him:
"Come in, my friend," and takes him by the arm.
"You must be weary," and sits him down inside the house.
For the blind man has long dreamed of having a friend
to share his lonely life.

The monster has never known kindness—the Baron was cruel—
but somehow he is able to accept it now,
and he really has no instincts to harm the old man,
for in spite of his awful looks he has a tender heart:
Who knows what cadaver that part of him came from?

The old man seats him at table, offers him bread,
and says, "Eat, my friend." The monster

26

rears back roaring in terror.
"No, my friend, it is good. Eat—gooood"
and the old man shows him how to eat,
and reassured, the monster eats
and says, "Eat—gooood,"
trying out the words and finding them good too.

The old man offers him a glass of wine,
"Drink, my friend. Drink—gooood."
The monster drinks, slurping horribly, and says,
"Drink—gooood," in his deep nutty voice
and smiles maybe for the first time in his life.

Then the blind man puts a cigar in the monster's mouth
and lights a large wooden match that flares up in his face.
The monster, remembering the torches of the villagers,
recoils, grunting in terror.
"No, my friend, smoke—gooood,"
and the old man demonstrates with his own cigar.
The monster takes a tentative puff
and smiles hugely, saying, "Smoke—gooood,"
and sits back like a banker, grunting and puffing.

Now the old man plays Mendelssohn's "Spring Song" on the violin
while tears come into our dear monster's eyes
as he thinks of the stones of the mob, the pleasures of mealtime,
the magic new words he has learned
and above all of the friend he has found.

It is just as well that he is unaware—
being simple enough to believe only in the present—
that the mob will find him and pursue him
for the rest of his short unnatural life,
until trapped at the whirlpool's edge
he plunges to his death.

Puppet Show

by Fredric Brown

Humanity is put to the test in this science-fiction classic. Can we get along with creatures from other worlds—any creatures at all?

Horror came to Cherrybell at a little after noon on a blistering hot day in August.

Perhaps that is redundant; *any* August day in Cherrybell, Arizona, is blistering hot. It is on Highway 89, about 40 miles south of Tucson and about 30 miles north of the Mexican border. It consists of two filling stations, one on each side of the road to catch travelers going in both directions, a general store, a beer-and-wine-license-only tavern, a tourist-trap-type trading post for tourists who can't wait until they reach the border to start buying serapes and huaraches, a deserted hamburger stand, and a few 'dobe houses inhabited by Mexican-Americans who work in Nogales, the border town to the south, and who, for God knows what reason, prefer to live in Cherrybell and commute, some of them in Model T Fords. The sign on the highway says, CHERRYBELL, POP. 42, but the sign exaggerates; Pop died last year—Pop

Anders, who ran the now deserted hamburger stand—and the correct figure should be 41.

Horror came to Cherrybell mounted on a burro led by an ancient, dirty and gray-bearded desert rat of a prospector who later gave the name of Dade Grant. Horror's name was Garvane. He was approximately nine feet tall but so thin, almost a stick-man, that he could not have weighed over a hundred pounds. Old Dade's burro carried him easily, despite the fact that his feet dragged in the sand on either side. Being dragged through the sand for, as it later turned out, well over five miles hadn't caused the slightest wear on the shoes—more like buskins, they were—which constituted all that he wore except for a pair of what could have been swimming trunks, in robin's-egg blue. But it wasn't his dimensions that made him horrible to look upon; it was his *skin*. It looked red, raw. It looked as though he had been skinned alive, and the skin replaced raw side out. His skull, his face, were equally narrow or elongated; otherwise in every visible way he appeared human—or at least humanoid. Unless you count such little things as the fact that his hair was a robin's-egg blue to match his trunks, as were his eyes and his boots. Blood red and light blue.

Casey, owner of the tavern, was the first one to see them coming across the plain, from the direction of the mountain range to the east. He'd stepped out of the back door of his tavern for a breath of fresh, if hot, air. They were about a 100 yards away at that time, and already he could see the utter alienness of the figure on the led burro. Just alienness at that distance, the horror came only at closer range. Casey's jaw dropped and stayed down until the strange trio was about 50 yards away, then he started slowly toward them. There are people who run at the sight of the unknown, others who advance to meet it. Casey advanced, slowly, to meet it.

Still in the wide open, 20 yards from the back of the little tavern, he met them. Dade Grant stopped and dropped the rope by which he was leading the burro. The burro stood still and dropped its head. The stick-man stood up simply by planting his feet solidly and standing, astride the burro. He stepped one leg across it and stood a moment, leaning his weight against his hands on the burro's back, and then sat down in the sand. "High gravity planet," he said. "Can't stand long."

"Kin I get water fer my burro?" the prospector asked Casey. "Must be purty thirsty by now. Hadda leave water bags, some other things, so it could carry—" He jerked a thumb toward the red-and-blue horror.

Casey was just realizing that it *was* a horror. At a distance the color combination seemed only mildly hideous, but close up—the skin was rough and seemed to have veins on the outside and looked moist (although it wasn't) and *damn* if it didn't look just like he had his skin peeled off and put back on inside out. Or just peeled off, period. Casey had never seen anything like it and hoped he wouldn't ever see anything like it again.

Casey felt something behind him and looked over his shoulder. Others had seen now and were coming, but the nearest of them, a pair of boys, were ten yards behind him. *"Muchachos,"* he called out. *"Agua por el burro. Un pozal. Pronto."*

He looked back and said, "What—? Who—?"

"Name's Dade Grant," said the prospector, putting out a hand, which Casey took absently. When he let go of it it jerked back over the desert rat's shoulder, thumb indicating the thing that sat on the sand. "*His* name's Garvane, he tells me. He's an extra something or other, and he's some kind of minister."

Casey nodded at the stick-man and was glad to get a nod in return instead of an extended hand. "I'm Manuel Casey," he said. "What does he mean, an extra something?"

The stick-man's voice was unexpectedly deep and vibrant. "I am an extraterrestrial. And a minister plenipotentiary."

Surprisingly, Casey was a moderately well-educated man and knew both of those phrases; he was probably the only person in Cherrybell who would have known the second one. Less surprisingly, considering the speaker's appearance, he believed both of them.

"What can I do for you, sir?" he asked. "But first, why not come in out of the sun?"

"No, thank you. It's a bit cooler here than they told me it would be, but I'm quite comfortable. This is equivalent to a cool spring evening on my planet. And as to what you can do for me, you can notify your authorities of my presence. I believe they will be interested."

Well, Casey thought, by blind luck he's hit the best man for his purpose within at least 20 miles. Manuel Casey was half Irish, half Mexican. He had a half-brother who was half Irish and half assorted-American, and the half-brother was a bird colonel at Davis-Monthan Air Force Base in Tucson.

He said, "Just a minute, Mr. Garvane, I'll telephone. You, Mr. Grant, would you want to come inside?"

"Naw, I don't mind sun. Out in it all day ever' day. An' Garvane here, he ast me if I'd stick with him till he was finished with what he's gotta do here. Said he'd gimme somethin' purty vallable if I did. Somethin'— a 'lectrononic—"

"An electronic battery-operated portable ore indicator," Garvane said. "A simple little device, indicates presence of a concentration of ore up to two miles, indicates kind, grade, quantity and depth."

Casey gulped, excused himself, and pushed through the gathering crowd into his tavern. He had Colonel Casey on the phone in one minute, but it took him another four minutes to convince the colonel that he was neither drunk nor joking.

Twenty-five minutes after that there was a noise in the sky, a noise that swelled and then died as a four-man helicopter set down and shut off its rotors a dozen yards from an extraterrestrial, two men, and a burro. Casey alone had had the courage to rejoin the trio from the desert; there were other spectators, but they still held well back.

Colonel Casey, a major, a captain, and a lieutenant who was the helicopter's pilot all came out and ran over. The stick-man stood up, all nine feet of him; from the effort it cost him to stand you could tell that he was used to a much lighter gravity than Earth's. He bowed, repeated his name and the identification of himself as an extra-terrestrial and a minister plenipotentiary. Then he apologized for sitting down again, explained why it was necessary, and sat down.

The colonel introduced himself and the three who had come with him. "And now, sir, what can we do for you?"

The stick-man made a grimace that was probably intended as a smile. His teeth were the same light blue as his hair and eyes.

"You have a cliché, 'Take me to your leader.' I do not ask that. In fact, I *must* remain here. Nor do I ask that any of your leaders be brought here to me. That would be impolite. I am perfectly willing for you to represent them, to talk to you and let you question me. But I do ask one thing.

"You have tape recorders. I ask that before I talk or answer questions you have one brought. I want to be sure that the message your leaders eventually receive is full and accurate."

"Fine," the colonel said. He turned to the pilot. "Lieutenant, get on

31

the radio in the whirlybird and tell them to get us a tape recorder faster than possible. It can be dropped by para—No, that'd take longer, rigging it for a drop. Have them send it by another helicopter." The lieutenant turned to go. "Hey," the colonel said. "Also 50 yards of extension cord. We'll have to plug it in inside Manny's tavern."

The lieutenant sprinted for the helicopter.

The others sat and sweated a moment and then Manuel Casey stood up. "That's a half–an-hour wait," he said, "and if we're going to sit here in the sun, who's for a bottle of cold beer? You, Mr. Garvane?"

"It is a cold beverage, is it not? I am a bit chilly. If you have something hot—?"

"Coffee, coming up. Can I bring you a blanket?"

"No, thank you. It will not be necessary."

Casey left and shortly returned with a tray with half-a-dozen bottles of cold beer and a cup of steaming coffee. The lieutenant was back by then. Casey put the tray down and served the stick-man first, who sipped the coffee and said, "It is delicious."

Colonel Casey cleared his throat, "Serve our prospector friend next, Manny. As for us—well, drinking is forbidden on duty, but it was 112 in the shade in Tucson, and this is hotter and also is *not* in the shade. Gentlemen, consider yourselves on official leave for as long as it takes you to drink one bottle of beer, or until the tape recorder arrives, whichever comes first."

The beer was finished first, but by the time the last of it had vanished, the second helicopter was within sight and sound. Casey asked the stick-man if he wanted more coffee. The offer was politely declined. Casey looked at Dade Grant and winked and the desert rat winked back, so Casey went in for two more bottles, one apiece for the civilian terrestrials. Coming back he met the lieutenant arriving with the extension cord and returned as far as the doorway to show him where to plug it in.

When he came back, he saw that the second helicopter had brought its full complement of four, besides the tape recorder. There were, besides the pilot who had flown it, a technical sergeant who was skilled in its operation and who was now making adjustments on it, and a lieutenant-colonel and a warrant officer who had come along for the ride or because they had been made curious by the *request* for a tape recorder to be rushed to Cherrybell, Arizona, by air. They were standing gaping at the stick-man and whispered conversations were going on.

The colonel said, "Attention" quietly, but it brought complete silence. "Please sit down, gentlemen. In a rough circle. Sergeant, if you rig your mike in the center of the circle, will it pick up clearly what any one of us may say?"

"Yes, sir. I'm almost ready."

Ten men and one extraterrestrial humanoid sat in a rough circle, with the microphone hanging from a small tripod in the approximate center. The humans were sweating profusely; the humanoid shivered slightly. Just outside the circle, the burro stood dejectedly, its head low. Edging closer, but still about five yards away, spread out now in a semicircle, was the entire population of Cherrybell who had been at home at the time; the stores and the filling stations were deserted.

The technical sergeant pushed a button and the tape recorder's reel started to turn. "Testing . . . testing," he said. He held down the rewind button for a second and then pushed the playback button. "Testing . . . testing," said the recorder's speaker. Loud and clear. The sergeant pushed the rewind button, then the erase one to clear the tape. Then the stop button.

"When I push the next button, sir," he said to the colonel, "we'll be recording."

The colonel looked at the tall extraterrestrial, who nodded, and then the colonel nodded at the sergeant. The sergeant pushed the recording button.

"My name is Garvane," said the stick-man, slowly and clearly. "I am from a planet of a star which is not listed in your star catalogs, although the globular cluster in which it is one of 90,000 stars is known to you. It is, from here, in the direction of the center of the galaxy at a distance of over 4000 light-years.

"However, I am not here as a representative of my planet or my people, but as minister plenipotentiary of the Galactic Union, a federation of the enlightened civilizations of the galaxy, for the good of all. It is my assignment to visit you and decide, here and now, whether or not you are to be welcomed to join our federation.

"You may now ask questions freely. However, I reserve the right to postpone answering some of them until my decision has been made. If the decision is favorable, I will then answer all questions, including the ones I have postponed answering meanwhile. Is that satisfactory?"

'Yes," said the colonel. "How did you come here? A spaceship?"

"Correct. It is overhead right now, in orbit 22,000 miles out, so it revolves with the earth and stays over this one spot. I am under observation from it, which is one reason I prefer to remain here in the open. I am to signal it when I want it to come down to pick me up."

"How do you know our language so fluently? Are you telepathic?"

"No, I am not. And nowhere in the galaxy is any race telepathic except among its own members. I was taught your language for this purpose. We have had observers among you for many centuries—by *we*, I mean the Galactic Union, of course. Quite obviously, I could not pass as an Earthman, but there are other races who can. Incidentally, they are not spies, or agents; they have in no way tried to affect you; they are observers and that is all."

"What benefits do we get from joining your union, if we are asked and if we accept?" the colonel asked.

"First, a quick course in the fundamental social sciences which will end your tendency to fight among yourselves and end or at least control your aggressions. After we are satisfied that you have accomplished that and it is safe for you to do so, you will be given space travel, and many other things, as rapidly as you are able to assimilate them."

"And if we are not asked, or refuse?"

"Nothing. You will be left alone; even our observers will be withdrawn. You will work out your own fate—either you will render your planet uninhabited and uninhabitable within the next century, or you will master social science yourselves and again be candidates for membership and again be offered membership. We will check from time to time and if and when it appears certain that you are not going to destroy yourselves, you will again be approached."

"Why the hurry, now that you're here? Why can't you stay long enough for our leaders, as you call them, to talk to you in person?"

"Postponed. The reason is not important but it is complicated, and I simply do not wish to waste time explaining."

"Assuming your decision is favorable, how will we get in touch with you to let you know *our* decision? You know enough about us, obviously, to know that *I* can't make it."

"We will know your decision through our observers. One

condition of acceptance is full and uncensored publication in your newspapers of this interview, verbatim from the tape we are now using to record it. Also of all deliberations and decisions of your government."

"And other governments? We can't decide unilaterally for the world."

"Your government has been chosen for a start. If you accept, we shall furnish the techniques that will cause the others to fall in line quickly—and those techniques do not involve force or the threat of force."

"They must be *some* techniques," said the colonel wryly, "if they'll make one certain country I don't have to name fall into line without even a threat."

"Sometimes the offer of reward is more significant than the use of a threat. Do you think the country you do not wish to name would like your country colonizing planets of far stars before they even reach the moon? But that is a minor point, relatively. You may trust the techniques."

"It sounds almost too good to be true. But you said that you are to decide, here and now, whether or not we are to be invited to join. May I ask on what factors you will base your decision?"

"One is that I am—was, since I already have—to check your degree of xenophobia. In the loose sense in which you use it, that means fear of strangers. We have a word that has no counterpart in your vocabulary: it means fear of and revulsion towards *aliens*. I—or at least a member of my race—was chosen to make the first overt contact with you. Because I am what you would call roughly humanoid—as you are what I would call roughly humanoid—I am probably more horrible, more repulsive, to you than many completely different species would be. Because to you I am a caricature of a human being, I am more horrible to you than a being who bears no remote resemblance to you.

"You may think you *do* feel horror at me, and revulsion, but believe me, you have passed that test. They *are* races in the galaxy who can never be members of the federation, no matter how they advance otherwise, because they are violently and incurably xenophobic; they could never face or talk to an alien of any species. They would either run screaming from him or try to kill him instantly. From watching

35

you and these people"—he waved a long arm at the civilian population of Cherrybell not far outside the circle of the conference—"I know you feel revulsion at the sight of me, but believe me, it is relatively slight and certainly curable. You have passed that test satisfactorily."

"And are there other tests?"

"One other. But I think it is time that I—" Instead of finishing the sentence, the stick-man lay back flat on the sand and closed his eyes.

The colonel started to his feet. "What in *hell?*" he said. He walked quickly around the mike's tripod and bent over the recumbent extra-terrestrial, putting an ear to the bloody-appearing chest.

As he raised his head, Dade Grant, the grizzled prospector, chuckled. "No heartbeat, colonel, because no heart. But I may leave him as a souvenir for you and you'll find much more interesting things inside him than heart and guts. Yes, he is a puppet whom I have been operating, as your Edgar Bergen operates his—what's his name?—oh yes, Charlie McCarthy. Now that he has served his purpose, he is deactivated. You can go back to your place, Colonel."

Colonel Casey moved back slowly. *"Why?"* he asked.

Dade Grant was peeling off his beard and wig. He rubbed a cloth across his face to remove makeup and was revealed as a handsome young man. He said, "What he told you, or what you were told through him, was true as far as it went. He is only a simulacrum, yes, but he is an exact duplicate of a member of one of the intelligent races of the galaxy, the one toward whom you would be disposed— if you were violently and incurably xenophobic—to be most horri- fied by, according to our psychologists. But we did not bring a real member of his species to make first contact because they have a phobia of their own, agoraphobia—fear of space. They are highly civilized and members in good standing of the federation, but they never leave their own planet.

"Our observers assure us you don't have *that* phobia. But they were unable to judge in advance the degree of your xenophobia, and the only way to test it was to bring along something in lieu of someone to test it against, and presumably to let him make the initial contact."

The colonel sighed audibly. "I can't say this doesn't relieve me in one way. We could get along with humanoids, yes, and we will when we have to. But I'll admit it's a relief to learn that the master race of the galaxy is, after all, human instead of only humanoid. What is the second test?"

"You are undergoing it now. Call me—" He snapped his fingers. "What's the name of Bergen's second-string puppet, after Charlie McCarthy?"

The colonel hesitated, but the tech sergeant supplied the answer. "Mortimer Snerd."

"Right. So call me Mortimer Snerd, and now I think it is time that I—" He lay back flat on the sand and closed his eyes just as the stick-man had done a few minutes before.

The burro raised its head and put it into the circle over the shoulder of the tech sergeant.

"That takes care of the puppets, Colonel," it said. "And now, what's this bit about it being important that the master race be human or at least humanoid? What is a master race?"

The Bottle Imp

by Robert Louis Stevenson & Adele Thane

*Robert Louis Stevenson wrote a tale of fantasy and
wish-fulfillment that has made generations of readers
ask: What price would I pay to have my wishes granted?
This play was based on Stevenson's story.*

SPANISH GENTLEMAN	LEI QUEEN
SPANISH LADY	SEVEN LEI DANCERS,
GYPSY WOMAN	*male and female*
ITALIAN GENERAL	DOCTOR
ARTIST	MOKO, *Lopaka's cousin*
KEAWE, *Hawaiian sailor*	RANDALL
LOPAKA, *his shipmate*	TURI, *servant woman*
OLD MAN	BEGGAR WOMAN
KOKUA, *Keawe's wife*	BOSUN, *Tahitian sailor*

SCENE ONE

TIME: *1600.*
SETTING: *A street in Spain.*

BEFORE RISE: *Spanish music is played, then fades. Sound of gong is heard.* SPANISH GENTLEMAN *enters.*

GENTLEMAN [*nervously*]: Any minute now, my beloved will pass by here. I'd give ten years of my life, if only she loved me as I love her! [SPANISH LADY *enters.*] Senorita? [LADY *stops.* GENTLEMAN *goes down on one knee before her.*] I can wait no longer. [*Fervently*] I adore you, and wish to make you my wife.

LADY [*haughtily*]: Never! Your attentions are unwelcome. I wouldn't marry you if you were the only man in Spain! [*Stalks off left. In despair,* GENTLEMAN *rises, starts left.* GYPSY WOMAN *enters right.*]

GYPSY: Young gentleman! [GENTLEMAN *stops, turns.*] I will read your palm for a centimo. Only one centimo, sir, to learn your future.

GENTLEMAN [*listlessly*]: My future isn't worth even that much, but what else have I to do? [*Gives her coin.*] Here you are.

GYPSY [*taking his palm and studying it*]: Ah! You are in love with a lady who does not return you affections, isn't that so?

GENTLEMAN [*surprised*]: Si! Si! That is true.

GYPSY: Would you like to make her your wife?

GENTLEMAN: More than anything! But, alas, she does not care for me.

GYPSY: But she might. [*Taking oddshaped bottle from pocket of skirt*] Do you see this bottle? An imp lives inside it, and he can grant your wish.

GENTLEMAN [*scoffing*]: Nonsense! I don't believe you!

GYPSY: But this is no ordinary bottle, sir. The glass of which it is made was tempered in the flames of hell! Any man who buys the bottle has the imp within it at his command. The imp will get him anything he desires—fame, riches, love!

GENTLEMAN: If that bottle can do all you say, doesn't it cost a fortune?

GYPSY: Once it did, but not now. You see, this bottle can be sold only for less money that it was bought for. The price has been falling over the years.

GENTLEMAN: I see. What is the price now?

GYPSY: Two hundred gold florins. [*Persuasively*] Surely the love of your lady is worth that!

GENTLEMAN [*eagerly*]: Si, it is worth that, and more. [*Unties money pouch at his waist and hands it to* GYPSY.] Take these coins. [*Gong* *sounds.* SPANISH LADY *reenters left, gazing ardently at* GENTLEMAN.]

GYPSY [*indicating* LADY]: Now that the bottle is yours, your lady has returned. She can resist your charms no longer. [GYPSY *exits.* LADY *crosses to* GENTLEMAN.]

LADY [*ardently*]: My dearest, what a fool I've been to turn you away. [*Taking his hands in hers*] I feel as though I've suddenly come to my senses. [*Tenderly*] If you would still have me, I would be honored to become your wife. [GENTLEMAN *beams, kisses her hand fervently, and they exit, arm-in-arm. Blackout to indicate passage of time.*]

> TIME: *1700.*
>
> SETTING: *A cafe in Italy.*
>
> BEFORE RISE: *Italian opera or other music to indicate setting is played, then fades. Gong is heard. Lights up on* GENERAL *and* ARTIST, *seated at a small table.* GENERAL *is holding bottle.*

ARTIST: General, I am delighted that you will consent to sell me your precious bottle, but I must confess that I am surprised, too. Think of all the battles it has helped you win!

GENERAL: Yes, but I am tired of war, and I am growing old.

ARTIST: Why don't you ask the imp in the bottle to let you live forever?

GENERAL: That's the only thing the imp cannot do. [*Impatiently*] Quick—I have no time to waste. Have you brought the money?

ARTIST: Yes, indeed—one hundred lira. [*He gives* GENERAL *bag of coins in exchange for bottle.*] Now I shall be the greatest artist in Italy since Michelangelo!

> [*Blackout to indicate passage of time.* GENERAL *and* ARTIST *exit.*]

> TIME: *1900.*
>
> SETTING: *Just outside of San Francisco. A painted backdrop shows hills of the city.*
>
> BEFORE RISE: *Hawaiian sailors,* KEAWE *and* LOPAKA, *enter left, in uniform.*

LOPAKA [*panting*]: Wait, Keawe! It's ridiculous for us to spend our leave in San Francisco climbing hills!

KEAWE: But look at the mansions, Lopaka! [*Pointing right*] How I'd love to own a house like that one! The steps shine like silver, and the windows are as bright as diamonds.

[OLD MAN *enters right.*]

OLD MAN: Good day, sailors. [*Proudly*] I noticed that you were admiring my little house.

KEAWE: It's very beautiful, sir.

OLD MAN [*mysteriously*]: That house and the garden and all my fortune came out of a bottle no bigger than a pint.

KEAWE: What? [*Laughs.*] A fairy tale!

LOPAKA [*to* KEAWE, *whispering*]: This man is daft! Let's go, Keawe!

KEAWE [*whispering*]: No, no, he's harmless, I'm sure. [*To* OLD MAN] I'd like to see that bottle.

OLD MAN [*taking bottle from pocket*]: Here it is. [*Slyly*] Now, if this bottle were yours, the imp inside it would give you anything you desired, merely for the asking.

KEAWE [*wistfully*]: I could get a house back in Hawaii and marry my sweetheart, Kokua.

LOPAKA: I could have a schooner. . . I've always wanted one.

KEAWE [*doubtfully*]: But how do I know what you say is true?

OLD MAN: I'll prove it to you. How much money do you have?

KEAWE [*checking his pockets*]: Fifty dollars.

OLD MAN: Give it to me, take the bottle, and wish your fifty dollars back into your pocket.

LOPAKA: Don't risk it, Keawe!

OLD MAN: There is no risk. If it doesn't happen, I'll return your friend's money to him. [KEAWE *gives money to* OLD MAN, *who pockets it, then hands him the bottle.*]

KEAWE: Imp of the bottle, I want my fifty dollars back! [*Gong is heard.* KEAWE *reaches into pocket, gasps in amazement, and takes out money.*] Look, Lopaka, my fifty dollars!

OLD MAN: There are more things about the bottle that you should know. Once it's yours, you can never be rid of it except by selling it, and you must sell it for less than you paid for it, or it will come back to you. If the bottle is still in your possession when you die, you face the flames of hell.

KEAWE [*shocked, thrusting bottle at* OLD MAN]: Here, take back your infernal bottle! There's nothing on Earth I want so much that I'm willing to endure the fires of hell.

OLD MAN: But all you have to do is to use the power of the imp in moderation, then sell it to someone else, and live out your life in comfort.

KEAWE [*shaking his head, emphatically*]: No, thank you! I don't want this bottle anymore. Take it back.

OLD MAN [*craftily*]: I can't do that. You've bought it for less than I paid for it. The bottle imp is yours now, and I wish you luck with it. [OLD MAN *exits briskly, right.*]

LOPAKA: Now you've done it!

KEAWE [*crossing right*]: Well, I won't keep the bottle. [*Tosses bottle off right.*] There! Let's go before the old man discovers it. [*As* KEAWE *and* LOPAKA *start off left, gong sounds.* KEAWE *stops, exclaims, and feels in his pocket.*]

LOPAKA: What's the matter?

KEAWE: The bottle! [*Holds up bottle.*] It's in my pocket again!

LOPAKA: It can't be! You left it in the old man's garden.

KEAWE: I see the old man was right when he said the only way I could get rid of the bottle was to sell it. [*Takes bottle from pocket.*] I'm beginning to believe it *is* magic! If I'm going to be stuck with it, I might as well make a wish.

LOPAKA: What will you wish for?

KEAWE: A beautiful house and garden in Hawaii, overlooking Kona Bay, and enough money so that I'll never have to work again. Then I'll sell the bottle and marry my sweetheart, Kokua.

LOPAKA: I'll buy the bottle from you for forty-nine dollars, and wish for a schooner for myself. I'll set up my own trading business. We'd better start for Hawaii, and see if your dream house is ready. [*They exit, left. Curtain.*]

SCENE TWO

TIME: *One year later.*
SETTING: *Garden of* KEAWE'S *house in Hawaii. At left is the veranda. A garden bench is center. A low wall stands before a painted backdrop of mountains and a volcano.*
AT RISE: KEAWE *enters from veranda and goes to look at view beyond wall.* LOPAKA *enters from right. Both are dressed in native Hawaiian costumes.*

LOPAKA [*calling*]: Hello, Keawe!

KEAWE [*coming downstage*]: Good to see you again, Lopaka. It's been nearly a year, hasn't it?

LOPAKA: And what a year it has been! We returned from San Francisco to find your uncle had died and left you this house in his will.

KEAWE: And up until then, I'd never even known I'd had an uncle.

LOPAKA [*knowingly*]: Keawe, you know it was all the doing of the bottle imp. Which is how I came to own a three-masted schooner.

KEAWE [*smiling*]: I hear you are about to set sail to Samoa on a trading voyage. [LOPAKA *nods.*]

LOPAKA: Tell me, how is your beautiful wife, Kokua? Have you told her about the bottle imp?

KEAWE [*troubled*]: No, and I never shall. What became of the bottle?

LOPAKA: As soon as I had my schooner, I sold it to my cousin Moko in Honolulu. [*Shaking* KEAWE'S *hand, warmly*] I must be off. May you be happy in your house, Keawe!

KEAWE: And you have a fortunate voyage. Aloha, my friend!

[LOPAKA *exits.* KOKUA *enters left from veranda.*]

KOKUA: Good morning, my husband. [KEAWE *goes to meet her.*]

KEAWE [*happily*]: Kokua, my love! Come, sit here with me and enjoy our garden. [*They sit on bench. Sound of Hawaiian music is heard from offstage.* KOKUA *rises and looks out at audience.*]

KOKUA: The village has begun the Lei Day celebration.

KEAWE [*rising*]: Ah, look, Kokua. I see the Lei Day Queen and her attendants are coming to welcome us to our new home. [*They watch as* LEI QUEEN *and seven* LEI DANCERS *enter to music at rear of auditorium, walk down aisle shaking gourds, and go on stage.* LEI QUEEN *adorns* KEAWE *and* KOKUA *with leis of red flowers.*]

LEI QUEEN: We greet you, lord and lady of the Great House. May you live in peace and harmony until the end of your days. Long life to you!

[*If desired,* LEI QUEEN *and* DANCERS *may perform a hula dance. At conclusion, they exit up aisle of auditorium.* KEAWE *and* KOKUA *return to bench, as* KOKUA *staggers and cries out.* KEAWE *catches her and seats her on bench.*]

KEAWE: Kokua! What is the matter? Are you ill?

KOKUA: I felt a sharp pain in my head.

KEAWE: I'll go for the doctor.

KOKUA: It's probably just a headache, but I think I'll go inside and lie down.

[KEAWE *helps* KOKUA *toward veranda as lights dim to blackout. Recorded music is heard during pause to indicate passage of time. When lights come up,* KEAWE *is seated on the bench, his head bowed.* DOCTOR *enters from veranda, carrying medial bag.*]

KEAWE [*springing up*]: Doctor, how is my wife?

DOCTOR: No better, Keawe—nor will she ever be, I'm sorry to say. Kokua has a strange fever for which I know no cure. I will return this evening, though there's little I can do. [*Sympathetically*] I'm very sorry, Keawe. [DOCTOR *exits.*]

KEAWE [*in despair*]: Oh, Kokua, Kokua, the light of my life! I cannot bear to lose you. If only I could do something! [*Pauses, then with sudden realization*] But I can! The bottle imp! I'll buy the bottle back again and ask the imp to cure Kokua. [*Hesitates.*] Lopaka said he sold the bottle to his cousin Moko in Honolulu. Maybe he still has it. I must go to Honolulu at once. [*He exits. Curtain.*]

SCENE THREE

TIME: *A short while later.*

SETTING: *A street in Honolulu.*

AT RISE: *Lights come up on* KEAWE *and* MOKO.

KEAWE [*desperately*]: So you see, Moko, I must buy the bottle back to cure my wife. Do you still have it?

MOKO [*regretfully*]: No, I sold it to Li-Po, an art dealer in the Chinese quarter.

KEAWE: I'll go there. [KEAWE *starts off.*]

MOKO [*calling*]: Wait, Keawe. [KEAWE *turns.*] Li-Po no longer has the bottle. He sold it to Kalamake the beachcomber, who in turn sold it to an Englishman—Randall—from the big island.

KEAWE: From Hawaii? Thank you, Moko. I am very grateful.

[KEAWE *walks out of spotlight, which fades.* MOKO *exits. Spotlight comes up left, revealing* RANDALL, *a haggard young man, staring dully at bottle on small table.*]

RANDALL: You cursed bottle! Nobody will buy you! I'm doomed!

KEAWE [*stepping into light, seeing bottle*]: The bottle imp—at last! Mr. Randall, I've come to buy that bottle.

RANDALL [*reeling back*]: To *what?*

KEAWE: To buy the bottle. What is the price?

RANDALL: It cost me—two cents!

KEAWE [*aghast*]: Two cents! Then the price now is—one cent, and I can never sell it again.

RANDALL [*falling on his knees*]: Buy it, oh, please buy it! You can have all my fortune in the bargain! I was mad when I bought it at that price. I had embezzled a lot of money, and I would have gone to prison.

KEAWE: Give me the bottle. Rather than live without Kokua, I'll chance the fires of hell. Here is one cent. [*Pays* RANDALL *one cent, and* RANDALL *runs off left, laughing deliriously.* KEAWE *takes bottle from table.*] O bottle imp, find Kokua and make her well! [*Sound of gong. Spotlight fades out.*]

> TIME: *Several days later.*
> SETTING: *Same as Scene Two.*
> AT RISE: KOKUA *is seated on bench reading.* TURI *enters from veranda with shawl.*

TURI: The evening is cool, mistress. Here is your shawl. [*Puts shawl around Kokua's shoulders.*]

KOKUA: Thank you, Turi. I feel so much better that I scarcely need it. [*As* TURI *turns to leave*] Turi, have you noticed a change in your master? He used to be cheerful and carefree, but now he seems worried and depressed.

TURI: Yes, mistress, there is something lying heavy on his heart. What it is, I do not know.

> [KEAWE *enters from veranda and slowly walks to wall.* TURI *exits.*]

KOKUA [*going to* KEAWE]: Dear husband, what is troubling you? When we were first married, you were the happiest of men, but ever since my illness you have been sad and withdrawn. Am I the cause of your unhappiness? Are you tired of me?

KEAWE [*in tormented tone*]: Oh, Kokua, if only you knew what I have done for love of you!

KOKUA: Then tell me what it is! I must share all things with you, the bad as well as the good.

KEAWE [*taking her hand*]: I have been silent, because I wanted to spare you, dear wife, but now you shall know all. Then, at least, you will understand how much I love you—so much that I dared hell to cure you of your illness.

KOKUA [*alarmed*]: I don't understand! [*They sit on bench.*]

KEAWE: Before we were married, I came into possession of an extraordinary bottle. Inside the bottle there was an imp that could grant wishes. I wished for this house and a fortune, and then I sold the bottle.

KOKUA: Why didn't you keep it?

KEAWE: The bottle can only be sold for less than it was bought for, and anyone who dies still owning the bottle will burn in hell forever.

KOKUA: How awful!

KEAWE: When you became ill, I went in search of the bottle to buy it back again and ask the imp to cure you. By the time I found it, it had passed through many hands and had dropped a great deal in value.

KOKUA: How much did you pay for it?

KEAWE [*in agony*]: One cent! And now I am bound to the bottle imp for eternity.

KOKUA [*rising, excitedly*]: But there is hope, dear husband! Oh, why didn't you tell me all this before? You've been worrying because you bought the bottle for one cent.

KEAWE [*rising impatiently*]: I cannot sell it, don't you understand? There is no coin less than a cent.

KOKUA: Oh, yes, there is! All the world is not Hawaii. In France there is a coin called the centime. It takes five of them to make a cent.

KEAWE: Are you sure?

KOKUA: I've seen the coin myself. We'll go to the French islands, to Tahiti, as fast as a ship can carry us. There we can sell it for four centimes—or three, two, even one centime!

KEAWE: Let's leave at once, and we'll be rid of the infernal bottle imp for good! [*They hurry left onto veranda and exit as curtain closes.*]

SCENE FOUR

TIME: *Three months later.*

SETTING: *A path on the beach in Tahiti. A palm tree stands right. A bamboo gate, left, leads to house.*

AT RISE: KOKUA *enters, opens gate, and looks off right anxiously.* KEAWE *enters from right and crosses to* KOKUA *wearily. He carries bottle in cloth bag.*

46

KEAWE: No luck again today. We've been in Tahiti for three months and I haven't sold the bottle yet. People laugh at me when I offer them health and riches for four centimes.

KOKUA: You can't give up, Keawe. Think what it means.

KEAWE: I made the bargain, and I'll stick by it, but I want to end my days near the hills of my fathers, not in a strange land. Kokua, let's go home.

KOKUA: No, Keawe, we must stay and keep on trying.

KEAWE: Very well. [*Starts through gate*] Are you coming in?

KOKUA: Not yet. It's a pleasant evening. I'll take a walk along the beach. [KEAWE *exits.* KOKUA *sighs and looks off after him.*] Dearest Keawe, you risked your soul for me. If only I could save you in return! [*As* KOKUA *crosses toward right exit, an old* BEGGAR WOMAN *enters.*]

BEGGAR [*holding out wooden bowl*]: Give to the poor, pretty lady. [*Coughing*] I am sick and hungry. I have no money to buy food. [*Pleadingly*] A few pennies, pretty lady, a few centimes?

KOKUA [*struck with a sudden idea*]: Centimes! [*Taking purse from pocket*] My good woman, I will give you a gold franc if you will do something for me.

BEGGAR [*eagerly*]: Yes, yes, I'll do it!

KOKUA: The man who lives in that house [*Pointing off left*] has a bottle that I want very much. He won't sell it to me for personal reasons. He'll sell it to you, though, because he's anxious to get rid of it. It will cost only four centimes. [*Gives* BEGGAR *four coins.*] Bring the bottle to me and I'll buy it from you for three centimes. Then I'll give you this gold franc. Now go.

BEGGAR: Yes, yes! [BEGGAR *exits left.* KOKUA *waits under palm tree, pacing nervously and looking anxiously toward left exit.*]

KOKUA: What is taking her so long? She should have the bottle by now. [BEGGAR *reenters with bottle.*] Oh, thank heaven, here she comes!

BEGGAR: Here is the bottle, pretty lady!

KOKUA: Shh! Not so loud—he might hear you! Come over here. [BEGGAR *crosses right. As* KOKUA *gives* BEGGAR *three coins,* KEAWE *enters left, looks for* KOKUA. *Seeing her with the* BEGGAR, *he hides behind gate, watching.*] There you are, three centimes—now give me the bottle. [*Takes bottle.*] And here is your gold franc. You have done me a great service.

BEGGAR: Thank you, pretty lady. [*Exits right.*]

KOKUA [*regarding bottle sadly*]: A love for a love, Keawe, and now mine is equal to yours. [KEAWE *exits quickly, unseen, then calls from offstage.*]

KEAWE [*from off left*]: Kokua! Kokua! [KOKUA *hides bottle in pocket of dress.* KEAWE *reenters.*] I've sold the bottle! An old woman bought it while you were out.

KOKUA [*embracing him*]: Now you are a free man!

KEAWE: Come, let's go into town and celebrate.

KOKUA: You go on alone, Keawe. I'm tired after my walk. I'm going to bed. You don't mind, do you?

KEAWE: Of course not. I won't stay long. [KOKUA *exits left.*] You think I don't know your secret! You sent the old woman to me, but I wormed the truth out of her. Two can play at that game. [KEAWE *exits right. Lights dim briefly to indicate passage of time.* KEAWE *and* BOSUN *enter, singing sea chanty.*] Come along, my fine sailing friend. I was a sailor once myself.

BOSUN: You, a sailor? You said you were a rich man, that you had a bottle or some such foolishness.

KEAWE: That's right—the bottle made me rich. My wife has it in the house. Help me to get it from her. There will be as much money for you as you wish.

BOSUN [*roughly*]: If there's a bottle, let's have it.

KEAWE: This is a bottle with an imp of the devil in it. The imp will bring you anything you ask.

BOSUN: I don't believe you.

KEAWE: It's true. You can see how rich I am, and what fine clothes I wear. [*Handing him coins*] Here are two centimes. Go to my wife and offer her these for the bottle. She'll be glad to sell it to you. Then bring the bottle to me and I will buy it from you for one centime. [*Giving* BOSUN *a push*] Now, go—and take care you don't breathe a word to my wife that I sent you. [BOSUN *exits.* KEAWE *hides behind palm tree, right. Sound of loud knocking is heard from off left.*]

BOSUN [*offstage*]: Ahoy! Hello in there! [*Knocking and shouting is repeated, then there is silence.* BOSUN *reenters.*] There's nobody home. Let's go back to town.

KEAWE: No, wait! My wife is coming out now. [*He dodges back behind tree.* KOKUA *enters, not seeing* KEAWE.]

KOKUA [*to* BOSUN, *timidly*]: Who are you? What are you doing here?

BOSUN: Good evening, ma'am. I've heard talk on the island that you have a magic bottle for sale, and I've come to buy it.

KOKUA [*surprised*]: Are you serious?

BOSUN [*belligerently*]: Look here, ma'am, I can't stand here all night. Are you goin' to sell me the bottle, or not?

KOKUA [*taking bottle from pocket*]: Do you have two centimes? That's the price of the bottle.

BOSUN [*gruffly*]: It must be mighty low on magic if it's as cheap as that, but here you are. [*Gives* KOKUA *coins and grabs bottle.*]

KOKUA [*gratefully*]: A kind god must have sent you.

BOSUN [*glancing toward tree and chuckling*]: Oh, he did, ma'am, he did! [*Smiling,* KOKUA *exits.* BOSUN *squints at bottle.*] It's a queer-lookin' thing. I'll try it. Come on, imp of Satan, fill my pockets with francs. [*Gong sounds.* BOSUN *jingles coins in pockets, takes out handful, and squeals with delight.*]

KEAWE [*coming out of hiding*]: Now you know I was speaking the truth. [*Holding out coin*] Here, sell me the bottle.

BOSUN [*jumping back*]: Hands off. Take another step near me and I'll cut your throat! You took me for a lunkhead, didn't you?

KEAWE [*astonished*]: What do you mean?

BOSUN: This is a pretty fine bottle, that's what I mean. How I got it for two centimes, I can't make out, but I'm sure I won't sell it to you for one!

KEAWE [*gasping*]: You mean you won't sell?

BOSUN: Not on your life!

KEAWE [*shaking him*]: But the devil made that bottle, and the man who has it when he dies will go to hell!

BOSUN [*laughs*]: That doesn't scare me! I reckon I'm goin' there anyway, and this bottle's the best thing to take me there that I've found yet. Fare-thee-well, matey! [BOSUN *exits right, whistling. With whoop of joy,* KEAWE *throws away coin, then runs toward gate.*]

KEAWE [*shouting*]: Kokua! Kokua! Start packing! We're going home! [*Exits. Curtain.*]

THE END

Bound to Bicker

by Laurence Steinberg

Do we control our own actions? Is some of what we do determined by the past—even the long-ago past of our evolutionary ancestors? Scientists have some intriguing answers.

"It's like being bitten to death by ducks." That's how one mother described her constant squabbles with her 11-year-old daughter. And she's hardly alone in the experience. The arguments almost always involve mundane matters—taking out the garbage, coming home on time, cleaning up the bedroom. But despite its banality, this relentless bickering takes its toll on the average parent's mental health. Studies indicate that parents of adolescents—particularly mothers— report lower levels of life satisfaction, less marital happiness and more general distress than parents of younger children. Is this continual arguing necessary?

For the past two years, my students and I have been examining the day-to-day relationships of parents and young teenagers to learn how and why family ties change during the transition from childhood into adolescence. Repeatedly, I am struck by the fact that, despite considerable love between most teens and their parents, they can't help sparring. Even in the closest of families, parents and teenagers squabble and bicker surprisingly often—so often, in fact, that we hear impassioned recountings of these arguments in virtually every discussion we have with parents or teenagers. One of the most frequently heard phrases on our interview tapes is, "We usually get along but. . . ."

As psychologist Anne Petersen notes in her article ("Those Gangly Years"), the subject of parent-adolescent conflict has generated considerable controversy among researchers and clinicians. Until about 20 years ago, our views of such conflict were shaped by psychoanalytic clinicians and theorists, who argued that spite and revenge, passive aggressiveness, and rebelliousness toward parents are all normal, even healthy, aspects of adolescence. But studies conducted during the 1970s on samples of average teenagers and their parents (rather than those who spent Wednesday afternoons on analysts' couches) challenged the view that family storm and stress was inevitable or pervasive. These surveys consistently showed that three-fourths of all teenagers and parents, here and abroad, feel quite close to each other and report getting along very well. Family relations appeared far more pacific than professionals and the public had believed.

Had clinicians overstated the case for widespread storm and stress, or were social scientists simply off the mark? The answer, just now beginning to emerge, seems to be somewhere between the two extremes.

The bad news for parents is that conflict, in the form of nagging, squabbling, and bickering, is more common during adolescence than during any other period of development, except, perhaps, the "terrible twos." But the good news is that arguments between parents and teenagers rarely undo close emotional bonds or lead adolescents and their parents to reject one another. And, although most families with adolescents go through a period of heightened tension, the phase is usually temporary, typically ending by age 15 or 16.

My own studies point to early adolescence—the years from 10 to 13—as a period of special strain between parents and children. But more intriguing, perhaps, is that these studies reveal that puberty plays a central role in triggering parent-adolescent conflict. Specifically, as youngsters develop toward physical maturity, bickering and squabbling with parents increase. If puberty comes early, so does the arguing and bickering; if it is late, the period of heightened tension is delayed. Although many other aspects of adolescent behavior reflect the intertwined influences of biological and social factors, this aspect seems to be directly connected to the biological event of puberty; something about normal physical maturation sets off parent-adolescent fighting. It's no surprise that they argue about overflowing trash cans, trails of dirty laundry, and blaring stereos. But why should teenagers going through puberty fight with their parents more often than youngsters of the same age whose physical development is slower? More to the point: If puberty is inevitable, does this mean that parent-child conflict is, too?

It often helps to look closely at our evolutionary relatives when we are puzzled by aspects of human behavior, especially when the puzzle includes biological pieces. We are only now beginning to understand how family relations among monkeys and apes are transformed in adolescence, but one fact is clear: It is common, at puberty, for primates living in the wild to leave their "natal group," the group into which they were born. Among chimpanzees, who are our close biological relatives, but whose family structure differs greatly from ours, emigration is restricted to adolescent females. Shortly after puberty, the adolescent voluntarily leaves her natal group and travels on her own—often a rather treacherous journey—to find another community in which to mate.

In species whose family organization is more analogous to ours, such as gibbons, who live in small, monogamous family groups, both adolescent males and females emigrate. And if they don't leave voluntarily soon after puberty begins, they are thrown out. In both cases, adolescent emigration helps to increase reproductive fitness, since it minimizes inbreeding and increases genetic diversity.

Studies of monkeys and apes living in captivity show just what happens when such adolescent emigration is impeded. For many nonhuman primates, the consequences can be dire: Among many species of monkeys, pubertal development is inhibited so long as youngsters remain in their natal group. Recent studies of monogamous or polyandrous monkeys, such as tamarins and marmosets, have shown that the sexual development of young females in inhibited specifically by their mothers' presence. When the mother is removed, so is her inhibitory effect, and the daughter's maturation can begin in a matter of a few days.

Taken together, these studies suggest that it is evolutionarily adaptive for most offspring to leave their family early in adolescence. The pressure on adolescents to leave their parents is most severe among primates such as gibbons, whose evolution occurred within the context of small family groups, because opportunities for mating within the natal group are limited and such mating may threaten the species' gene pool. It should come as no surprise, therefore, to find social and biological mechanisms that encourage the departure of adolescent primates—including, I think, humans—from the family group around puberty.

One such mechanism is conflict, which, if intense enough, drives the adolescent away. Squabbling between teenagers and their parents today may be a vestige of our evolutionary past, when prolonged proximity between parent and offspring threatened the species' genetic integrity.

According to psychologist Raymond Montemayor of Ohio State University, who studies the relationships of teenagers and their parents, accounts of conflict between adolescents and their elders date back virtually as far as recorded history. But our predecessors enjoyed an important advantage over today's parents: Adolescents rarely lived at home much beyond puberty. Prior to industrialization in this country, high school-aged youngsters often lived in a state of semiautonomy in which they were allowed to work and earn money but lived under the authority of adults other than their parents. Indeed, as historian Michael Katz of the University of Pennsylvania notes, many adolescents actually were "placed out" at puberty—sent to live away from their parents' household—a practice that strikingly resembles the forced emigration seen among our primate relatives living in the wild.

Most historians of adolescence have interpreted the practice of placing out in terms of its implications for youngsters' educational and vocational development. But did adolescents have to leave home to learn their trade? And is it just coincidental that this practice was synchronized with puberty? Historian Alan Macfarlane notes that placing out may have developed to provide a "mechanism for separating the generations at a time when there might otherwise have been considerable difficulty" in the family.

Dozens of nonindustrialized societies continue to send adolescents away at puberty. Separating children from their parents, known as "extrusion," has a great deal in common with the behavior of many non-human primates. In societies that practice extrusion, youngsters in late childhood are expected to begin sleeping in households other than their parents'. They may see their parents during the day but are required to spend the night with friends of the family, with relatives, or in a separate residence reserved for preadolescents. Even in traditional societies that do not practice extrusion formally, the rite of passage at puberty nevertheless includes rituals symbolizing the separation of the young person from his or her family. The widespread existence of these rituals suggests that adolescent emigration from the family at puberty may have been common in many human societies at some earlier time.

Conflict between parents and teenagers is not limited to family life in the contemporary United States. Generally, parent-child conflict is thought to exist at about the same rate in virtually all highly developed, industrialized Western societies. The sociological explanation for such intergenerational tension in modern society is that the rapid social change accompanying industrialization creates irreconcilable and conflict-provoking differences in parents' and children's values and attitudes. But modernization may well have increased the degree and pervasiveness of conflict between young people and their parents for other reasons.

Industrialization hastened the onset of puberty, due to improvements in health, sanitation, and nutrition. (Youngsters in the United States go through puberty about four years earlier today than their counterparts did 100 years ago.) Industrialization also has brought extended schooling, which has prolonged youngsters' economic dependence on their parents and delayed their entrance into full-time work roles. The net result has been a dramatic increase over the past century in the amount of time that physically mature youngsters and their parents must live in close contact.

A century ago, the adolescent's departure from home coincided with physical maturation. Today, sexually mature adolescents may spend seven or eight years in the company of their parents. Put a different way, industrialization has impeded the emigration of physically mature adolescents from their family of origin—the prescription for parent-adolescent conflict.

Puberty, of course, is just one of many factors that can exacerbate the level of tension in an adolescent's household. Inconsistent parenting, blocked communication channels and extremes of strictness or permissiveness can all make a strained situation worse than it need be. An adolescent's family should seek professional help whenever fighting and arguing become pervasive or violent or when they disrupt family functioning, no matter what the adolescent's stage of physical development.

Given our evolutionary history, however, and the increasingly prolonged dependence of adolescents on their parents, some degree of conflict during early adolescence is probably inevitable, even within families that had been close before puberty began. Telling parents that fighting over taking out the garbage is related to the reproductive fitness of the species provides little solace—and doesn't help get the garbage out of the house, either. But parents need to recognize that quarreling with a teenager over mundane matters may be a normal—if, thankfully, temporary—part of family life during adolescence. Such squabbling is an atavism that ensures that adolescents grow up. If teenagers didn't argue with their parents, they might never leave home at all.

Interlocking Pieces

by Molly Gloss

Transplantation of organs has brought better health and longer life to many. In the future, as this science-fiction story suggests, the possibilities may be really amazing.

For Teo, there was never a question of abandoning the effort. After the last refusal—the last European Minister of Health sent her his personal explanation and regrets—it became a matter of patience and readiness and rather careful timing.

A uniformed policeman had been posted beside her door for reasons, apparently, of protocol. At eight-thirty, when he went down the corridor to the public lavatory, Teo was dressed and waiting, and she walked out past the nurses' station. It stood empty. The robo-nurse was still making the eight-o'clock rounds of the wing's seventy or eighty rooms. The organic nurse, just come on duty, was leaning over the vid displays in the alcove behind the station, familiarizing herself with the day's new admissions.

Because it was the nearest point of escape, Teo used the staircase. But the complex skill of descending stairs had lately deserted her, so she stepped down like a child, one leg at a time, grimly clutching the metal bannister with both hands. After a couple of floors she went in again to find a public data terminal in a ward that was too busy to notice her.

They had not told her even the donor's name, and a straightforward computer request met a built-in resistance: DATA RESTRICTED***KEY IN PHYSICIAN IDENT CODE. So she asked the machine for the names of organ donors on contract with the regional Ministry of Health, then a list of the hospital's terminal patients, the causes and projected times of their deaths, and the postmortem neurosurgeries scheduled for the next morning. And, finally, the names of patients about whom information was media-restricted. Teo's own name appeared on the last list. She should have been ready for that but found she was not, and she sat staring until the letters grew unfamiliar, assumed strange juxta-positions, became detached and meaningless—the name of a stranger.

The computer scanned and compared the lists for her, extrapo-lated from the known data, and delivered only one name. She did not ask for hard copy. She looked at the vid display a moment, maybe longer than a moment, and then punched it off and sat staring at the blank screen.

Perhaps not consciously, she had expected a woman. The name, a man's name, threw her off balance a little. She would have liked a little time to get used to the sound of it, the sound it made in her head and on her lips. She would have liked to know the name before she knew the man. But he would be dead in the morning. So she spoke it once, only once. Out loud. With exactness and with care. "Dhavir Stahl," she said. And then went to a pneumo-tube and rode up.

In the tube there were at first several others, finally only one. Not European, perhaps North African, a man with eyebrows in a thick straight line across a beetled brow. He watched her sidelong—clearly recognized her—and he wore a physician's ID badge. In a workplace as large as this one the rumor apparatus would be well established. He would know of her admission, maybe even the surgery that had been scheduled. Would, at the very least, see the incongruity of a VIP patient, street-dressed and unaccompanied, riding up in the public pneumo-tube. So Teo stood imperiously beside him with hands cupped together behind her back and eyes focused on the smooth center seam of the door while she waited for him to speak, or not.

When the tube opened at the seventy-eighth floor he started out, then half turned toward her, made a stiff little bow, and said, "Good health, Madame Minister," and finally exited. If he reported straightaway to security, she might have five minutes, or ten, before they reasoned out where she had gone. And standing alone now in the pneumo-tube, she began to feel the first sour leaking of despair— what could be said, learned, shared in that little time?

There was a vid map beside the portal on the ninety-first floor. She searched it until she found the room and the straightest route, then went deliberately down the endless corridors, past the little tableaux of sickness framed where a door here or there stood open, and finally to Stahl's door, closed, where there was no special feel of death, only the numbered code posted alongside the name to denote a life that was ending.

She would have waited. She wanted to wait, to gather up a few dangling threads, reweave a place or two that had lately worn through. But the physician in the pneumo-tube had stolen that possibility. So she took in a thin new breath and touched one thumb to the admit disk. The door hushed aside, waited for her, closed behind her. She stood just inside, stood very straight, with her hands open beside her thighs.

The man whose name was Dhavir was fitting together the pieces of a masters-level holoplex, sitting cross-legged, bare-kneed, on his bed, with the scaffolding of the puzzle in front of him on the bed table and its thousands of tiny elements jumbled around him on the sheets. He looked at Teo from under the ledge of his eyebrows while he worked. He had that vaguely anxious quality all East Europeans seem to carry about their eyes. But his mouth was good, a wide mouth with creases lapping around its corners, showing the places where his smile would fit. And he worked silently, patiently.

"I . . . would speak with you," Teo said.

He was tolerant, even faintly apologetic. "Did you look at the file, or just the door code? I've already turned down offers from a priest and a psychiatrist and, this morning, from somebody in narcotics. I just don't seem to need any deathbed comforting."

"I am Teo."

"What is that? One of the research divisions?"

"My name."

58

His mouth moved, a near smile, perhaps embarrassment.

"They hadn't told you my name, then."

And finally he took it in. His face seemed to tighten, all of it pulling back toward his scalp as the skin shrinks from the skull of a corpse, so that his mouth was too wide and there was no space for smiling. Or too much.

"They. . . seem to have a good many arbitrary rules," Teo said. "They refused me this meeting, your name even. And you mine, it appears. I could not—I had a need to know."

She waited raggedly through a very long silence. Her palms were faintly damp, but she continued to hold them open beside her legs. Finally Dhavir Stahl moved, straightened a little, perhaps took a breath. But his eyes stayed with Teo.

"You look healthy," he said. It seemed a question.

She made a slight gesture with one shoulder, a sort of shrugging off. "I have . . . lost a couple of motor skills." And in a moment, because he continued to wait, she added, "The cerebellum is evidently quite diseased. They first told me I would die. Then they said no, maybe not, and they sent me here. 'The state of the art,' or something to that effect."

He had not moved his eyes from her. One of his hands lightly touched the framework of the puzzle as a blind man would touch a new face, but he never took his eyes from Teo. Finally she could not bear that, and her own eyes skipped out to the window and the dark sheets of rain flapping beneath the overcast.

"You are . . . not what I expected," he said. When her eyes came round to him again, he made that near smile and forced air from his mouth—not a laugh, a hard sound of bleak amusement. "Don't ask! God, I don't know what I expected." He let go the puzzle and looked away finally, looked down at his hands, then out to the blank vid screen on the wall, the aseptic toilet in the corner. When he lifted his face to her again, his eyes were very dark, very bright. She thought he might weep, or that she would. But he said only, "You are Asian." He was not quite asking it.

"Yes."

"Pakistani?"

"Nepalese."

He nodded without surprise or interest. "Do you climb?"

She lifted her shoulders again, shrugging. "We are not all Sherpa bearers," she said with a prickly edge of impatience. There was no change at his mouth, but he fell silent and looked away from her. Belatedly she felt she might have shown more tolerance. Her head began to ache a little from a point at the base of the skull. She would have liked to knead the muscles along her shoulders. But she waited, standing erect and stiff and dismal, with her hands hanging, while the time they had went away quickly and ill used.

Finally Dhavir Stahl raised his arms, made a loose, meaningless gesture in the air, then combed back his hair with the fingers of both hands. His hair and his hands seemed very fine. "Why did you come?" he said, and his eyelashes drew closed, shielding him as he spoke.

There were answers that would have hurt him again. She sorted through for one that would not. "To befriend you," she said, and saw his eyes open slowly. In a moment he sighed. It was a small sound, dry and sliding, the sound a bare foot makes in sand. He looked at the puzzle, touched an element lying loose on the bed, turned it round with a fingertip. And round.

Without looking toward her, he said, "Their computer has me dead at four-oh-seven-fourteen. They've told you that, I guess. There's a two percent chance of miscalculation. Two or three, I forget. So anyway, by four-thirty—" His mouth was drawn out thin.

"They would have given you another artificial heart."

He lifted his face, nearly smiled again. "They told you that? Yes. Another one. I wore out my own and one of theirs." He did not explain or justify. He simply raised his shoulders, perhaps shrugging, and said, "That's enough." He was looking toward her, but his eyes saw only inward. She waited for him. Finally he stirred, turned his hands palms up, studied them.

"Did they—I wasn't expecting a woman. Men and women move differently. I didn't think they'd give a man's cerebellum to a woman." He glanced at Teo, at her body. "And you're small. I'm, what, twenty kilos heavier, half a meter taller? I'd think you'd have some trouble getting used to . . . the way I move. Or anyway the way my brain tells my body to move." He was already looking at his hands again, rubbing them against one another with a slight papery sound.

"They told me I would adapt to it," Teo said. "Or the . . . new cerebellum could be retaught."

His eyes skipped up to her as if she had startled or frightened him. His mouth moved too, sliding out wide to show the sharp edge of his teeth. "They didn't tell me that," he said from a rigid grin.

It was a moment before she was able to find a reason for his agitation. "It won't—They said it wouldn't . . . reduce the donor's . . . sense of self."

After a while, after quite a while, he said, "What word did they use? They wouldn't have said 'reduce.' Maybe 'correct' or 'edit out.'" His eyes slid sideways, away from her, then back again. His mouth was still tight, grimacing, shaping a smile that wasn't there. "They were at least frank about it. They said the cerebellum only runs the automatic motor functions, the skilled body movements. They said they would have expected—no, they said they would have liked—a transplanted cerebellum to be mechanical. A part, like a lung or a kidney. The 'mind' ought to be all in the forebrain. They told me there wouldn't be any donor consciousness, none at all, if they could figure out how to stop it."

In the silence after, as if speaking had dressed the wound, his mouth began to heal. In a moment he was able to drop his eyes from Teo. He sat with his long, narrow hands cupped on his knees and stared at the scaffolding of his puzzle. She could hear his breath sliding in and out, a contained and careful sound. Finally he selected an element from among the thousands around him on the bed, turned it solemnly in his hands, turned it again, then reached to fit it into the puzzle, deftly finding a place for it among the multitude of interlocking pieces. He did not look at Teo. But in a moment he said, "You don't look scared. I'd be scared if they were putting bits of somebody else inside my head." He slurred the words a little at the end and jumped his eyes white-edged to Teo.

She made a motion to open her hands, to shrug, but then, irresistibly, turned her palms in, chafed them harshly against her pants legs. She chose a word from among several possible. "Yes," she said. And felt it was she who now wore the armored faceplate with its stiff and fearful grin.

Dhavir's eyes came up to her again with something like surprise, and certainly with tenderness. And then Teo felt the door behind her, its cushioned quiet sliding sideways, and there were three security people, there, diminishing the size of the room with their small crowd, their turbulence. The first one extended her hand but did not quite touch Teo's arm. "Minister Teo," she said. Formal. Irritated.

Dhavir seemed not to register the address. Maybe he would remember it later, maybe not, and Teo thought probably it wouldn't matter. They watched each other silently, Teo standing carefully erect with her hands, the hands that no longer brushed teeth nor wrote cursive script, the hands she had learned to distrust, hanging open beside her thighs, and Dhavir sitting crosslegged amid his puzzle, with his forearms resting across those frail, naked knees. Teo waited. The security person touched her elbow, drew her firmly toward the door, and then finally Dhavir spoke her name. "Teo," he said. And she pulled her arm free, turned to stand on the door threshold, facing him.

"I run lopsided," he said, as if he apologized for more than that. "I throw my heels out or something." There were creases beside his mouth and his eyes, but he did not smile.

In a moment, with infinite, excruciating care, Teo opened her hands palms outward, lifted them in a gesture of dismissal. "I believe I can live with that," she said.

The Last Wolf

by Mary TallMountain

the last wolf hurried toward me
through the ruined city
and I heard his baying echoes
down the steep smashed warrens
of Montgomery Street and past
the few ruby-crowned highrises
left standing
their lighted elevators useless

passing the flicking red and green
of traffic signals
baying his way eastward
in the mystery of his wild loping gait
closer the sounds in the deadly night
through clutter and rubble of quiet blocks

I heard his voice ascending the hill
and at last his low whine as he came
floor by empty floor to the room
where I sat
in my narrow bed looking west, waiting
I heard him snuffle at the door and
I watched
he trotted across the floor

he laid his long gray muzzle
on the spare white spread
and his eyes burned yellow
his small dotted eyebrows quivered

Yes, I said.
I know what they have done.

Henry Martindale, Great Dane

by Miriam Allen deFord

Magical transformations have long been part of folktales and horror stories. They can be the basis of humorous fiction, as well.

What woke Lida was being hit on the nose with a pajama button. She opened her eyes abruptly. It was just barely light. She turned sleepily, took one look at the other side of the double bed, and let out a screech. The thing lying there opened its eyes—Henry's eyes—and said—in Henry's voice, "What's the matter, honey?"

It wasn't Henry, though. It was a Great Dane in Henry's pajamas, with the top buttons popped off by its barrel chest.

Lida shot out of bed. She got as far as the door before it occurred to her that she might be the one who had gone crazy. Trembling, she inched back and took another look.

It was a Great Dane, all right.

"I—I—you look like a dog!" she managed to gasp.

Henry—or whatever was there—took it calmly. Henry always took everything calmly.

"Are you just calling me a so-and-so in a nice way, or is something wrong with your eyes?"

Lida made a tremendous effort and pulled herself together. Ordinarily she was almost as calm as Henry.

"It isn't my eyes," she breathed. "Either I've lost my mind or something awful has happened to you. Look at yourself—uh—Henry, and tell me which it is."

Henry's myopic blue eyes inspected his arm—his foreleg—well, his upper limb.

"Can't see a thing without my glasses. Give them to me, honey. Something does feel funny. Bring me your hand-mirror, too."

The glasses wouldn't go on Henry's new broad nose. Lida held them with one shaking hand and passed over the mirror with the other. There was a long silence.

"You're not crazy, Lida," Henry said at last. "Something's happened."

Lida was speechless. Even Henry was shaken. He didn't drop the mirror, but he laid it down with a distinct thump. Perhaps that was because he had been holding it in the crook of his—limb. He no longer had an opposable thumb with which to grasp it. Unquestionably, what he now had was a large dog's paw.

"Shades of Kafka!" he said in an awed tone. "Thank God I didn't turn into a giant cockroach!"

"B-but what—"

"How do I know? Things do happen. I've been trying for years to get you to take Charles Fort seriously. He has records of stranger things than this."

Lida burst into tears.

"Now don't cry, honey." He put out a comforting paw, but she shrank from it involuntarily. Fortunately for his feelings, Henry didn't see that. His glasses had fallen off as soon as she let go of them.

"We'll have to figure things out and use our common sense," he said in the reasonable tone she had been listening to for eight years.

"C-common sense! What has common sense to do with this unbelievable, horrible—"

"Hysteria won't help. Horrible maybe, but not unbelievable because it has happened—and when a thing is real, we have to believe it."

He climbed laboriously out from under the bedclothes, hesitated a moment, his hind paws hovering over his slippers, then stood solidly on all fours. The pajama pants fell down. Solemnly he peered at himself in Lida's full-length pier glass.

"I can't get a good look this way. Find some adhesive tape and fasten my glasses on for me, will you, Lida? And take this pajama top off me. It's—it's inappropriate."

In a waking nightmare, Lida did as she was told. Henry took a long look.

"A Great Dane!" he murmured. "I wonder why. I never cared for them particularly. They cost too much to feed. Well, let's get down to cases."

He glanced helplessly at the pad and pencil which always stood on the night table on his side of the bed. Until this morning, Henry Martindale had been a reasonably prosperous radio and television script writer.

"I can't think without notes, Lida," he sighed. "Write down what I tell you and I'll try to reason this thing out. But put on your dressing-gown first, dear, or you'll freeze."

This evidence of husbandly concern transformed Lida's horror into passionate loyalty and love. Somewhere within this canine shape, her own Henry lived intact. Suppose it had happened to her instead? Suppose she had awakened to find herself a Pekinese or a Siamese cat or a parakeet? Could she doubt that Henry would have stood by her?

She reached for her dressing-gown, wrapped herself in it and took up the pad and pencil.

At his dictation, she began to write the first considered reflections of Henry Martindale, Great Dane.

"One," he began, "this is either temporary or permanent. If it is temporary, I may wake up as myself tomorrow morning. In any event, I can manage to wait for a week—with your cooperation, Lida—" She nodded and even contrived to smile. "For a week, without arousing suspicion. Call up everybody we had engagements with and tell them I have the flu. Tell Mrs. Whoozis the same thing when she comes to clean and keep her out of this room. I have a deadline on that story for Channel Twenty, but I can dictate it as usual and you can deliver it. You'd better do all the phoning, too. I could talk, but I doubt if I could hold the phone."

Lida hid her shudder. Henry went on dictating.

"Two—if this condition is permanent, if it isn't gone in a week or so, then it may mean that I must face my remaining life-span as a Great

Dane. Question—have I now the life expectancy of a human being or of a dog?

"I must then make a major decision: where and how can I live? I have earned my living for fifteen years now as a writer. I could continue to dictate my stories, of course, but it would be utterly impossible to conceal my—my present appearance. It would be still more impossible to explain it, even to such hardened sophisticates as the script editors and agency men for whom I write. As for the family—my brother and Aunt Agatha and your mother, Lida, and the rest of your relatives—I could, perhaps, brazen it out and make advantageous connections with a television program."

"I won't have that!" Lida burst out hotly. "I won't have you displaying yourself as a—as a freak!"

"An intelligent talking dog might be worth big money to the right sponsor," Henry said reasonably.

"No. They'd investigate first and—you couldn't get away with it anyway, Henry. Your eyes—they're still yours and people would wonder. And your voice—you've talked too often in public and on the air."

"Perhaps you're right—it might be too risky—even though it would have been rather fun. Well, then, if I'm stuck for an indefinite period with this—this phenomenon, there will be only one thing I can do. We must go somewhere where we know nobody, where you can be a widow who lives alone with only her dog for company." He paused. "Wait a moment, Lida. No, don't write this down. Maybe I'm assuming too much. I'm taking it for granted that you'll be with me. No, let me finish. If you feel you can't stand it—if you want to go away, I'll understand—I'd never blame you. And, Lida, I beg of you, don't stick by me out of a sense of duty, just because a dog without an owner—even a dog that can think and talk—is a lost dog. Just because . . ."

He had to stop. His throat had tightened too much for him to go on.

Lida's last vestige of horror left her. "Don't be a fool, darling," she said brusquely. "I married you, not your looks. *You're* still here. If we have to go to the ends of the earth—if I have to pretend forever that you're my pet Great Dane . . ." she gulped down a sob. "Just so we're together . . ."

"Bless you, dearest," Henry said quietly. He had recovered his usual calm. "Go on taking this down now. We won't have to go to the ends of the earth. We can find some secluded place in the country, perhaps not more than a hundred miles from here. We'll have to think of ways to fend off our families and friends. But I can dictate my stories to you and we can handle all my business contacts by mail. There will be difficulties, of course. How can I sign letters or endorse checks, for instance?"

"I can forge your signature. I've done it before on letters, when you were deep in a story and didn't want to be disturbed."

"Yes, that would work. And we'll find means to solve the other problems as they come up. All we need face now is a week of waiting to see if this—transformation is permanent."

A thought occurred to Lida. "About food, Henry," she suggested nervously. "Do you want to eat as usual or—or should I buy some Canine Delight?"

"Hm—that's a point." Henry let his mind dwell on ham and eggs, then on Canine Delight. "I'm sorry, dear," he said apologetically, "but I'm afraid you'd better lay in a supply of dog food."

"It's eight o'clock. The grocery at the corner will be open. I'll dress and go out to get some—some breakfast for you. And here—I'll fasten your glasses on firmly so you can read the paper while I'm gone."

Already, she discovered gratefully, she was becoming accustomed to the new Henry. Her hands were steady as she adjusted the tape. She restrained an impulse to stroke the tawny head.

Henry watched her leave, his large myopic blue eyes moist. He had not mentioned the fear that gnawed at him, a fear worse than the bite of hunger. Suppose this were an intermediate stage—suppose he should gradually become more dog and less man, lose his power of speech, his power of human thought?

Time enough to face that if it began to happen. Time, probably, to run away alone into the unknown before she could stop him. Fortunately, all they possessed was in their joint names and ultimately Lida would have to let him be declared dead and cash in on his sizable insurance.

He gazed unseeingly at the paper most of the time while she was gone. Nothing in it was as strange as what had happened to Henry Martindale.

The week went by somehow. Every night Henry went to sleep a Great Dane—he admitted he was more comfortable sleeping on a rug beside the bed—and every morning he woke up a Great Dane again. He ate Canine Delight and one night when Lida broiled two chops for herself, he enjoyed the juicy bones. But he felt no impulse to wag his tail or to bark. Inside, he was still completely Henry.

They devised a strap to hold his spectacles on, to avoid the pulling of hair that accompanied removing the adhesive tape. Physically, he was comfortable, though he began to long for exercise and fresh air. He could stand anything for a week—even Aunt Agatha's insistence that she must come to help nurse the poor boy, plus her resentment of Lida's firm refusal. Once there was a scare when the woman who came twice a week to clean insisted that she could vacuum the bedroom without bothering the invalid—but Lida won that round.

At the end of the week, it became obvious that the metamorphosis was either permanent or would be of indefinite duration. Henry had met his deadline and dictated the beginning of another story in his television series, but he felt distracted and uninterested.

"I guess this is it, Lida," he conceded on the eighth day. "We have to plan."

They pored over maps and made a list of upstate villages to be inspected.

"I can make the trips and come back and report to you," said Lida dubiously. "But I hate to leave you here all alone day after day. You could let the phone ring, but suppose Aunt Agatha came or Bill Goodlett or the Harrisons? Or a telegram or a special delivery letter?"

"I'll go with you," Henry decided promptly. "Call up all the likely people and tell them I'm better, but you're taking me to the country to recuperate. We'll write everybody later, when we've found a place, that we're going to stay for a while. But first you'd better buy me a dog collar and a leash, and then take me downtown and get a license for me."

"Oh, *darling!*"

"I know—it's grim. But we must be practical. I'll have to have a name, too. What do you want to call your Great Dane? Anything but Hamlet will suit me."

"Why can't you still be Henry?" asked Lida faintly.

"Well, I guess it wouldn't matter—where we're going, wherever that is, they wouldn't get the point. All right, register me as Henry. I'll sit in the back of the car, as a dog should. Thank goodness you can drive, honey. I'd hate to travel in a baggage car!"

So Lida, her huge dog in the back seat, began visiting rural real estate offices to inquire about secluded cottages for rent. There was no sense in tying up their capital by buying a house, when at any moment—as they still assured each other—this calamity might end and Henry be himself again.

All they got was turndowns. There was nothing, simply nothing, to be had. Villagers, they learned, don't rent their homes.

They had reached a state of dull despair when, almost the last on their hopeful list, they drove to Farmington.

Yes, said Mr. Bullis, there *was* one place—the old Gassingham house. It was in kinda bad shape, needed some work done and it was three miles from the highway. But Liz Gassingham—she was all that was left—she lived in town now and she refused to sell. She'd never said she'd rent, but she might.

Lida almost said she would take it sight unseen, but stopped herself in time.

"There is only one thing, Mrs. Martindale. That dog of yours . . ." He cast an unfriendly eye on Henry, lying peaceably on the floor of the real estate office.

"You mean Miss Gassingham wouldn't let me keep a pet?"

"Pet, yes—but pets to Liz is cats. She mightn't like the idea of a tenant with a dog—a monster dog like that, especially."

"But, Mr. Bullis, I told you—I'm all alone since my husband—went . . ." Lida's voice shook. "The doctors said I must go to the country to get back my strength. But I'd be afraid to live so far from people without Henry to protect me."

"That his name, Henry?"

Henry laid a warning paw on her foot. They had agreed that they must keep their own name because of the mail and she was remembering that most of the letters would be addressed to Henry.

"It's silly—perhaps you'll think it's crazy—but that was my husband's name. I—it makes me feel less lonely to call the dog Henry, too. He—went so suddenly."

"Um." Mr Bullis sounded disapproving. "Well, let's go see Liz. Put the mutt in your car. You might talk her over, but not if she saw him first. Funny-looking dog at that, if you don't mind my saying so—awful funny-looking eyes. Will he make a row if you leave him?"

"Oh, no, Henry never—Great Danes don't bark much."

70

"Better lock him in. If the kids spot him, they'll be all over him and you don't want him jumping out."

Henry settled down philosophically in the car and took a nap.

Lida came back triumphant.

"I told her you were a settled old dog, Henry, too lazy to do any damage," she announced. "And that you were clean and never had fleas and just loved cats."

"Good gosh!" said Mr. Bullis, staring. "You talk to that mutt just like he was human!"

Lida tried to smile it off. "That's what being alone does to people, Mr. Bullis."

The house was pretty dreadful. It was big and water-tight, but that was about all that could be said for it. Their modern furniture would look weird in it. The only lighting was by kerosene lamps. The water came from an outdoor pump—Henry wondered dismally if he could learn to pump with his mouth. The sanitary arrangements consisted of an outhouse in the back yard and the cooking had to be done on a wood stove, with a fireplace for central heating.

But they had to have it and they could get along somehow. At least, Mr. Bullis said, Lida could hire Ed Monahan to chop wood and do the heaviest chores and there was old Mrs. Sharp—she sometimes took in washing for the summer people and she might be willing to do Mrs. Martindale's household laundry. He looked disparagingly at Lida's city-bred slenderness.

A month later, all the lies had been told, all the arrangements had been made, and Lida and Henry were residents of Farmington.

It was pretty rugged. Henry had to be careful—and make sure his spectacles were off—whenever anyone came to the house. But they managed. His mind had never been working better and he dictated scripts like mad, till he had a good backlog in several agency inventories. Smith, of D.D.B. & I., wrote him that if rusticating for their health would add the same touch of originality and conviction to other writers' stuff, he'd recommend it to all his regulars. Henry twitched his ears irascibly when he read that one.

In a way, it was Lida who unwittingly brought on the inevitable crisis.

It was an evening in early November. She was sitting by the fireplace, knitting a sweater for Henry, who was lying contentedly at her feet. Henry had become almost reconciled to being a dog. It was nice not having to wear clothes, for instance, though when the really cold weather came, he would probably want the sweater. He wished he could help Lida more with the housework, but there aren't many household tasks that can be done without hands.

Suddenly Lida said, "Henry, I've been thinking."

"So I've noticed. What about?" he countered.

"I've been thinking about—it."

"It" was what they had tacitly agreed to call Henry's transmogrification.

"What's the use of thinking about it?"

"That's just what I mean. You're just taking it lying down."

Henry rose to his feet and looked at her apologetically.

"Don't be silly," she said impatiently. "I don't mean that way. I mean you've—you've just accepted it. You haven't tried to—oh, to think how or why it happened or whether there's any way to undo it."

"Did the swan that was found in Central Park try to figure out how it could become Dorothy Arnold again?" Henry inquired sententiously.

"I don't know what you're talking about."

"Fort—I'm a Fortean phenomenon. He never said anything about the possibility of reversal."

"That doesn't mean it couldn't happen."

"Perhaps not. My guess is it would have to be spontaneous. But if it will make you any happier, Lida, I'll try anything you suggest."

"Henry, don't you *want* to be human again?"

"Because *you're* human, yes. But selfishly, I confess, so long as I have the mind and the power of speech of a human being . . ."

"That's one of the things I've been wondering about. A dog's throat and mouth aren't formed for human speech, yet you can talk clearly with your own voice."

"I know. I've been puzzled about that, too. And my sight—dogs haven't very good sight, anyway, so that might fit. But they're supposed to be color-blind and I'm not any more than I ever was. I know very well that sweater you're knitting is beige and maroon."

"What about your other senses?"

"Well, I always had good hearing and I still have. But I certainly don't have the sense of smell of a dog—of other dogs, I mean."

"Don't say that!"

"I'm sorry. I get sort of confused sometimes. And there are other—disadvantages, of course. But, Lida, there's no use in going into all that. I don't know how to change it."

"Tell me, can you remember anything special about that night—the night before it happened?"

"I've tried. I remember I was working late on a script. It was nearly two when I went to bed and you were sound asleep. The last thing I recall was thinking, 'I'm dog-tired.' And then you woke me and it was morning and I was—like this."

"Dog-tired. Do you think . . ."

"Nonsense—pure coincidence. Or maybe . . ."

Henry felt sudden excitement thrill through him from head to tail. All his calm acceptance dropped from him as his pajamas once had done.

"Lida, I've just remembered! The story I was working on that night was the one about a werewolf who evolved from a primitive wolf-like creature instead of from apes, like us."

Lida stared at him. "You mean . . ."

"Could be. Perhaps that story wasn't just imaginary—perhaps I happened on actual facts and got transformed as a warning, maybe, or maybe that's how people turn into werewolves."

"Then there might be a way for you to change back again!"

"I don't see how. I didn't engineer it and I wouldn't know how to engineer the reversal. I'd have to get in touch somehow with a real werewolf. Hey, here's an idea! Let's get to work on another story about werewolves. It might be like—like tuning them in, if they really exist. And perhaps my transformer would get on my beam again. He might be glad to straighten me out."

"But suppose he isn't. *You're* not altogether sorry about being a dog—you just told me so. Suppose he decides you *like* being a pet, with no responsibilities."

"That's not fair, honey." Henry's tone was aggrieved. "Don't I work just as hard as I ever did?"

"Oh, darling. I didn't mean you—just him!"

"In that case, he won't want to change me back and everything will stay the way it is now. What else could he do to me?"

Henry began dictating the new werewolf script the next morning. It went fast and smoothly, as if something in him knew beforehand what to say.

Yet neither of them felt comfortable. He said nothing to Lida, but under the flow of words he was conscious of an inner struggle, as though something or somebody were trying vainly to impede them. And she, though the original incitement had been her own, grew increasingly nervous and apprehensive.

At the end of three hours, the script was half done and both of them were exhausted.

"Let's knock off for the rest of the day," Henry suggested. "We can go on with it tomorrow. We both need exercise. I'd like to explore those thick woods—the ones we've never gone into."

Nothing could have been more trim, tame, and civilized than Farmington. Yet not five miles from the village, in the back country, lay the last remnants of what was once virgin forest. Its trees were of no value as timber and it had a bad reputation. There were said to be wildcats there, even bears. Parts of it belonged to landowners who never bothered with it, parts were still in the public domain. Local stories made it the hideout of robbers in the past and children were disciplined by threats of taking them there and leaving them.

Lida took Henry's spectacles off him and put on his collar and leash. Passing through the village in the car, they encountered Liz Gassingham, who scarcely returned Lida's greeting and snorted at sight of Henry.

"Great, horrible thing!" she muttered, glaring. "If she ever lets it loose to hurt my kitties, I'll throw her out, lease or no lease!"

They parked the car at the end of the road and walked half a mile over fields to the edge of the wood. Once inside, Lida shrank back a little.

"Henry," she said, "do you think there really are wild animals here? Let's not go too far."

Henry couldn't smile any more, but he laid a protecting paw on her hand. "The Great Dane," he said soothingly, "was originally a boar-hound. I can handle anything we're likely to meet And we won't get lost—don't forget I have the canine sense of direction. I can't explain it, Lida, but all day I've felt impelled toward these woods," he added.

"Maybe something *is* going to happen here," said Lida hopefully. "Oh, darling, if it only would! You do want it, too, don't you?"

"I want us to be alike again, dearest."

They walked for an hour among the old trees and Henry ran

74

eagerly from tree to tree, sniffing. They startled woodchucks and squirrels, but nothing larger appeared. It was very quiet and peaceful and not too cold, even with the trees bare and patches of early snow left here and there on the ground from the first fall of the season. After a while, they found themselves climbing until the level floor of the woods had become a hill.

Suddenly Henry darted through some underbrush toward a depression in the hillside, behind the bulk of a huge uprooted tree.

"You know," he called back in a voice that shook a little, "this could be dug out to make a good snug cave. I could do it myself with my paws."

"What of it? You don't want to live in a cave, do you?"

"I suppose not." The excitement deserted him. "I'm all confused. There was something very important I was thinking about and now I seem to have forgotten it completely."

"Poor Henry, you're tired. Let's go back. I'm tired, too."

"I guess it was all nonsense about werewolves, after all," said Henry in the car. "Well, it's a pretty good story, anyway. The agency ought to eat it up. You know, darling, I just remembered—vampires turn people they bite into their own kind. Why not werewolves?"

"But you're a weredog," said Lida absently. Then, sharply, "Henry, you wouldn't!"

"Just one little nip, darling—after we get home, of course."

When rent day came around, Lida didn't turn up at Liz Gassingham's house.

Mrs. Sharp had a whole washing ready that Lida never called for.

Ed Monahan went out to chop wood, but found nobody home.

Mail piled up in the post office and the postmistress noted, as so often before, that most of it was addressed to the deceased Mr. Martindale. Why, she wondered loudly, didn't the woman tell his friends he had passed away—or deserted her, more likely? Something funny there!

But nobody moves fast in Farmington and over a week passed before a delegation, led by Mr. Bullis, went out to investigate.

The door was unlocked and the house was empty.

Everything was in order, with the table laid for breakfast and the stove stuffed with wood and paper, ready to light.

The bed had been slept in and at its foot, where apparently that dog slept on a rug, lay a white flannel nightgown frivolously printed with sprigs of roses. All its buttons were off.

The rest of Lida's usual house attire lay over the back of a chair. Her shoes were beneath it, a pair of pink bedroom slippers beside the bed.

In the living room, they found a partly knitted maroon-and-beige sweater, evidently intended for the dog, and beside the typewriter a pile of manuscripts.

Nobody ever saw Lida Martindale again.

It was a year from the following summer that two adventurous boys from the village, egging each other on, raided the big woods. They came back, pale and frightened, to report that they had seen the dog that used to belong to Mrs. Martindale. It had emerged from the thick underbrush, they said, where the slope of the ground began to climb the hill. It had gone back to the wild, the boys claimed, and they had been lucky to get away without harm.

"You might have been killed. Somebody ought to go out there and shoot the thing," Mr. Bullis asserted.

"Aw," said the older of the two, aged fifteen, looking a bit sick, "it wasn't doing nobody no hurt. Nobody hardly ever goes there anyhow. I know I ain't going no more."

"There was a she-dog too, just like him, and some puppies," the younger boy blurted out.

"Shut up!" growled the older. "You want folks to think you're crazy? Jim was so scared, he got to seeing things, Mr. Bullis. There wasn't nothing there 'cept that big mutt of Mrs. Martindale's."

"I wasn't scared," Jim retorted. He caught his friend's eye and added hastily, "But I could of made a mistake."

"You must have, my boy," said Mr. Bullis kindly. "That dog was a Great Dane and there's never been another anywhere around here that I ever heard of."

"You idiot!" The fifteen-year-old scolded when the two boys were alone again. "Don't you ever open your yap about that again. They'd put us both in the booby-hatch."

They kept far away from the woods after that and gradually they became convinced that they must have been out of their heads for a while. How *could* a dog have yelled, "Scram, you kids, or do you want me to bite?"

The Pits Beneath the World

by Mary Gentle

Pel can't understand. The Talinorian was her friend, not her stalker. Why can't extraterrestrials have the same values we do?

Awind stirs the blue grass of the Great Plains. The flat land stretches out to the perfect circle of the horizon. There is not a rock or tree to break the monotony. Seventeen moons burn in a lilac sky. A blue-giant sun is setting, its white dwarf companion star hangs in the evening sky.

The small figure stands waist-deep in the grass. She aches from running bent over in a crouch. Now she straightens, biting back a gasp at the pain.

Shrill chittering and whistling noises come from the distance. Seen!

Up until today she's been sorry that she's small for her age. Now she's glad. Only a small human could lie concealed in the Plains grass. She edges away and crawls on, hands and knees stained blue by the grass sap.

Behind her, the whistling of the Talinorian hunting party begins again.

There is no doubt: she is their quarry.

When did it go wrong? Pel Graham wondered. The Talinorians are our friends. What happened?

She was hurt and bewildered as well as afraid.

It had all been fine until two days ago . . .

There!—the Talinorian whistled—The *chelanthi!*—

Pel peered ahead between its sheaf of stalked eyes. Far out across the Great Plain, grass rippled where no wind blew.

"Hold on!" Called Pel's mother, riding high astride the glittering carapace of another Talinorian, Baltenezeril-lashamara.

With a clatter of shell the Talinorian hunting party edged down the side of the cliff. Pel clung as Dalasurieth-rissanihil lurched under her, body-suckers clutching the rock as they moved down the almost vertical surface. The long segmented body rippled.

"Faster!" she yelled, and then remembering that the human voice had too low a frequency for the Talinorian's sensors, tapped the message out on the alien's eye-carapace. The stalked eyes retreated briefly under the hard shell. Pel had learned to interpret this as amusement.

Now they went more slowly. The Talinorians were better suited to rocky cliffs and scarps. Only for the traditional *chelanthi* hunts did they venture down onto grassland.

Pel waved to her mother, and to the other members of the Earth scientific expedition honored to ride in the Talinorian hunt. It was a time of relaxation. They must have finished negotiating, Pel thought, not very interested. She did not want to leave Talinor yet.

The wind blew her hair in her eyes. She turned her head, seeing the rocky "coast" behind them. Clusters of rock rose starkly out of the flat grassland. It was impossible to think of them as anything but islands, jutting out of a grass ocean. On the rocking-gaited Talinorian, Pel felt like a ship at sea. Hunting the beasts of the ocean, the *chelanthi.*

—We're falling behind—

The other unburdened Talinorians were faster. Dalasurieth-rissanihil slowed still further.

The "islands" they had left were small, and in a natural condition.

78

They were covered with bush-berry-trees, the purple fruit hanging down in long strings; and with the *cureuk* flowers that folded up when touched. Mothbirds flew only in this hour between the blue sun's rising and the white sun's following, when they again roosted. A multitude of singing insects nested in the crevices of the rock, and the nights were bright with luminous starflies. It was different from Talinor-Prime, Pel thought, where the expedition had set down the shuttle.

—They have made a kill—

—Where?—

Pel stared ahead over Dalasurieth-rissanihil's carapace, but saw nothing in detail. If she admitted the truth she preferred riding to hunting, and wasn't sorry to miss the end.

A wisp of smoke coiled up ahead.

—Dala', look!—

—Stray laserbeam. Don't they realize what a grass fire might do?— Dalasurieth-rissanihil sounded, as far as she could tell, furious.

—I thought you had to use spears?—

—Tradition demands it. The leader will have something to say to them back at Prime!—

Pel saw the Talinorians put the fire out before it could spread. Others carried the scaly *chelanthi* slung across their patterned carapaces, held in place by their forked scorpion-tails. Clusters of thin jointed arms waved excitedly.

—Will you stay for the hunt tomorrow?—

—I have to go home. It's my—. The click and whistle language failed her.—It's a party. The northern team should be back. And besides, it's my . . .—

She couldn't find a word for "birthday," and struggled to make it clear. Dalasurieth-rissanihil rattled its forked tail.

—So you will have been alive eleven seasons of your home world? That is a long time to be adult. I had thought you younger—

Privately she laughed. Aliens were often stupid about the most obvious things. Except, she thought, I don't suppose it is obvious to them; not even an eleventh birthday...

—How old are you, Dala'?—

—I have been adult three seasons—

Pel couldn't be bothered to translate that into Earth-standard years. She knew it wasn't long.

—Yes, but how long ago were you born? I mean, I'm not adult. Not exactly. I don't come of age until I'm fourteen—

—You are not adult?—

—No, not yet; I told you. Oh, you don't understand—

They were turning back towards the islands and Talinor-Prime. Dalasurieth-rissanihil was unusually silent on the way back across the plain, and she wondered if she had offended him.

Talinor-Prime. An "island" in a grassland "ocean," but this island was a continent. Big enough to take a flyer three days to cross it. A rock plateau a few meters higher than the surrounding plain, and with a totally different ecology—as Pel's xeno-biologist mother was very prone to telling her. More important from Pel's point of view, Talinor-Prime held the city and the starship landing-field.

It was noon before they arrived. The two suns—blue Alpha and white Beta—blazed together in the sky. Pel had a black and a purple shadow following her on the carved rock walkway.

"Ready for the party tomorrow?" her mother asked.

"You bet. Are the others back yet?"

"Not yet. I'm expecting them to call in soon."

The long arthropod bodies of the Talinorians glided past them on low trollies. Some preferred the powered walkways that riddle the rock of Prime. They were too low for an adult human to enter without stooping, but Pel was small enough to stand upright in them.

They turned down another walkway and saw the starfield between the wasp-nest dwellings of the Talinorians. Pel looked through the view-grills as they walked. She liked the inside of the "nests," with their powered valve-doors and beam-operated equipment. Talinorian manip-ulative limbs weren't strong, but they were good at delicate work. Their great love was glass, which their formulae made stronger than any-where else in the galaxy. Sculptured, woven in filaments, blown into spheres and cubes and octagons, the ornaments glittered in the light of the two suns; and Talinor-Prime chimed as the wind blew.

"Pel!"

Pel ran out from staring through a view-grill. She caught up as they began to walk across the vast expanse of the starfield. The blue-gray rock was hot underfoot.

"Tell me," her mother said, "what do you and Dala' talk about?"

80

"Oh . . . things," Pel shrugged.

"I'm sorry in a way that there are no other kids with this expedition. I always wonder if it's fair to bring you on these trips. But since there are just the two of us . . ."

Pel made a rude noise. "Try and stop me coming with you," she invited. "Anyway, it's training—for the future."

Her mother laughed.

The starfield was on a long spit of "island" jutting out into the grassland. At that time there were no other sharp ships there. Pel looked at the squat dirty shuttle with affection. It would be great to have the other half of the team back with the ship.

I wonder if they brought me any presents? she thought; and didn't answer when her mother asked her what she was grinning at.

Blue Alpha's dawn light stretched her shadow far behind her on the rocks. The morning smelled clean, spicy. A cool wind blew out of the south. Pel scrambled down the long spit towards the edge of the grassland. Mothbirds beat their fragile wings round her, bright against the amethyst sky.

She could just have waited on the shuttle. But Pel preferred to keep watch in the open, and wait for the ship's return.

Something whirred past her ear.

She swatted at it automatically. Glancing round, she saw some Talinorians on the slope above her, and recognized one of them as Dalasurieth-rissanihil.

A shadow flicked her face.

The spear clattered on the rock beside her.

Pel sprang up. The red line of a laser kicked the rock into molten steam. While she watched, Dalasurieth-rissanihil raised the gun and took aim again.

She took a flying leap off the rocks, running as fast as she could through the grass. It slowed her, but she managed to reach the cover of a rock overhang.

Another party of Talinorians waited beyond it.

She swerved out into the open, running like a hare. Arms and legs pumping, lungs burning; she fell into a stride that took her far out into the blue grassland.

It dawned on her as she fell into the scant cover that the grass afforded, far from Talinor-Prime, that those first shots had not been meant to kill. Only to start her running. Only to force her out into the grass ocean, where killing might take place honorably with glass-tipped hunting spears.

She put her head down, gripped her knees, and tried to stop shaking. When the first panic subsided, bewilderment remained. Then it hardened into a cold determination.

Pel Graham looked back to the distant cliffs of Prime. She thought, Somehow I'll get back. I'll make them pay. Somehow I'll find out . . . Dalasurieth-rissanihil—*why*?

She heard the hunting party in the distance.

Evening found her still further away, driven out of sight of Prime. The islands were specks on the horizon. If it had not been for the gentle ridges and undulations of the ground here, she would have been spotted long ago. Now she clung to cover under an alien sky. The grassland went from aquamarine to azure to indigo as Beta set.

The expedition will come looking, Pel thought. I only have to stay free until the shuttle flies over and finds me. I bet they're already on their way—

The grass rustled.

Pel flopped down on her stomach. A blunt muzzle pushed along through the reed-bladed grass. A *chelanthi*. Its low flexible body was covered in mirror-scales, camouflaging it. She saw tiny eyeclusters almost hidden under the muzzle. The actual mouth was further back, between the front pairs of legs. As she watched, it began to crop the grass.

Aren't they meat-eaters? Pel wondered.

A scaly hide brushed her arm. She shot back, biting off a yell. The *chelanthi* raised its muzzle, eye-stalks wavering reproachfully. Pel stifled laughter. It scuttled off past the first *chelanthi*. She followed it.

The ridge concealed a dip beyond. The hollow was pitted with holes, among which many *chelanthi* were grazing. They seemed harmless. They probably were . . .

Another *chelanthi* emerged from one of the pits. They must burrow deep, Pel thought. How else would they hide from the Talinorians?

A long whistle sounded through the gathering twilight. She thought, what if the hunters have heat-seeking equipment? That'll show up human body-heat miles off when it's dark . . .

Pel Graham grinned. It was a crazy idea she had. Good, but crazy;

still, she might be a little crazy herself by now. There was every excuse for it.

The *chelanthi* did not object when Pel crept into one of the pits beside them. It was dry, earth trodden down hard, and surprisingly roomy. She lay sheltered among their warm scaly bodies, hidden from anything on the grassland above.

The blue sun set in an ocean-colored sky. The few stars of the galaxy's rim burned in lonely splendor. The moons rose, all seventeen of Talinor's satellites. Sometimes their varying orbits made them appear in clusters, but now they hung in a string of crescents. Pel Graham slept fitfully in the warm night. The Talinorian hunting party passed five miles to the west.

Morning came chill. Disturbed out of one pit when the *chelanthi* went to graze, Pel crawled into another. It had only one occupant. This *chelanthi* made a racheting noise like a broken clock and nipped at her hand. Pel backed out in an undignified scramble.

She watched. The *chelanthi* was busy at the mouth of that pit. It appeared to be stringing a substance from glands under its body. The stubby forepaws gripped the pit's mouth, and Pel saw that it was beginning to weave a web over it.

She listened, but heard no sound of the hunt.

I'm safe here. At least I'm hidden. But I have to get back to Prime. I have to warn them!

The day wore on. Pel was extremely bored by the *chelanthi*. True, they did her no harm. They did nothing except crop the grass. The webbed pit remained closed, and she was not sure if the *chelanthi* inside were sleeping, hibernating, or dead. Hourly the mass of its hidden body became more shapeless.

Unless the Talinorians stumbled across her, the *chelanthi* would hide her. They camouflaged her against long-distance night sensors, and in the day radiation from the two suns made long-distance sensing impossible.

It was not until then that it occurred to her; if she was hidden from Talinorian sensors, she must also be hidden from those of the Earth expedition.

The second evening came. The blue giant Alpha eclipsed the white dwarf Beta as the suns set. Pel was hungrier than she had ever thought it possible to be. Thirst made her drink the water that collected on the flat-bladed grass, and hope that it didn't carry infection.

She was even more determined to get back to Talinor-Prime. It was think of that, or panic, and she didn't dare panic.

The *chelanthi* gave up grazing and headed for the pits.

Pel thought about the webbed pit, she hadn't looked at it in a while. She walked over to it.

As she watched, the webbing over the pit's entrance twitched. It bulged as if something beneath it were trying to get out. Pel stepped back rapidly.

The webbing reared up and split. Something sharp, gray, and glistening protruded. It twitched again, slitting the web still further. A multitude of thin, many-jointed and hard-shelled limbs followed, gripping the sides of the pit. A carapace emerged. Under it, clustered eye-stalks waved. The body heaved itself up onto the grass, segment by armored segment, disclosing the suckers on the underside. The patterned shell gleamed. Last to leave the pit was the forked scorpion-tail.

Pel stared.

The young Talinorian looked round at the grass-eating *chelanthi*, at Pel Graham who stood frozen with astonishment, and clicked and whistled softly. As it scuttled off it said—Don't you know that there are some things it's better for you not to see?—

It changes everything! Pel thought.

The grass was harsh under her hands and knees. She followed the line of a low ridge. The pits and the broken web were far behind her. She knew that the new-born Talinorian would betray her to the hunting party as soon as it found them.

White Beta rose, and the plains flooded with color. A little warmth came back to Pel as she moved.

It spoke, it was a *chelanthi*, and it—changed.

It had looked very like Dalasurieth-rissanihil, who was only three seasons "adult."

Shrilly in the distance came the whistle of the hunters. Abandoning the *chelanthi,* she had abandoned safety.

I will get back to Prime! she told herself.

She saw something flash in the morning sky like a thrown coin.

"Hey! Hey, shuttle!"

They'll never hear me, never see me, never sense me... If there was any way I could mark myself out ...

Fire would have been best, but she had no way to set the grass lands on fire. And then she remembered the *chelanthi* hunt.

Deliberately Pel stood up and ran to the crown of the ridge. She waved both arms over her head, semaphoring wildly.

The shrilling of the hunters was louder, much louder.

As fleet as fear could make her, she ran. A laserbeam licked redly out to her left, and even through her exhaustion she had time for a grin of triumph.

A line of grass burst into crackling fire. The shuttle's course veered wildly. It began to descend.

Pel could hardly breathe. The world was going red and black round her. But she staggered over the ramp a hundred yards ahead of her pursuers and fell into her mother's arms.

The Talinorian hunting party dwindled below.

"That took some sorting out. You musn't blame them," Pel's mother turned away from the computer console. "It's not uncommon in nature to have a larval stage, after all. Even on Earth, moths and butter-flies ... And until they change they're quite unintelligent. Just animals, really."

"Did you tell them?" Pel asked. "About—children?"

Outside the shuttle's viewport, Talinor-Prime sparkled in the light of two suns. The wind ruffled the grasslands.

"It's a great step forward in understanding each other." She put her hand on Pel's shoulder. "You see, when you said you weren't adult—"

"They thought it was all right to hunt me down?"

"Don't be bitter. Worlds are different places." She turned her back. "If they'd hurt *you* ..."

Pel knew what that note in her mother's voice meant. Lightly she said, "I'm all right."

"I know you are, love."

But you don't understand, she thought. Dalasurieth-rissanihil was my friend ...

"Were you afraid? Oh, that's a stupid question ... it was a brave thing you did, Pel."

"Will they stop the hunting?"

"You don't have to be afraid. Not now it's been made clear to everyone."

"No." Pel shook her head impatiently. "The *chelanthi* hunting. Will you stop that?"

"You know we can't interfere in alien worlds." Her mother sat down at the console. "You get some rest. I'm going to pilot us in."

The door irised shut. Back in the main body of the shuttle, Pel stared out of the port. Hunger, exhaustion; she has been told that these will pass.

Two suns cast the descending shuttle's double shadow on the landing-field. She remembers the endless grassland like a great sea.

She remembers Talinor-Prime jutting up in headlands and cliffs and peaks. And she remembers the pits beneath the world, and the *chelanthi* as they nuzzled at her in their sleep.

She sits down and hides her face in her hands.

Pel Graham is thinking of the other children.

How to Be Great!
What Does It Take to Be a Hero?

by the Editors of *Psychology Today*

What makes a man or woman heroic? This essay describes the qualities that heroes share—and why heroes are important.

John F. Kennedy had it, Bill Clinton doesn't. John Wayne personified it, but Sylvester Stallone comes up short. Martin Luther King, Jr.? Certainly. But Colin Powell remains a question mark.

We're talking about heroism. Greatness. That special something that wins you admiration, adoration, and maybe even your face on a postage stamp.

Heroes may seem passé in a cynical era where we seem to relish tearing down icons more than we do creating new ones or cherishing the ones we already have. Some folks, moreover, find the very idea of heroes objectionable, arguing that there's something elitist about exalting individuals who, after all, are nothing more than flesh and blood, just like the rest of us.

But we sorely need heroes—to teach us, to captivate us through their words and deeds, to inspire us to greatness. And if late 20th-century America seems in short supply of them, the good news is that the pool of potential heroes has never been greater. That's because every one of us—ourselves, our friends, even our kids—has heroic potential. And there is plenty we can do to develop that untapped greatness, to ensure that the next generation gets the heroes it needs.

PORTRAIT OF A HERO

Though our personal heroes differ, we all share a common vision of what a hero is—and isn't. Temple University psychologist Frank Farley, Ph.D., has distilled this vision into what he calls his "5–D" model of greatness. Together the five "D's" help explain what makes a hero, where they come from, and why they're so important.

The first "D" is for *determinants,* six character traits Farley believes define the essence of heroism. Not every hero has them all. But the more you have, the better. So if you seek greatness, either in yourself or your children, you would do well to nurture these aspects of personality.

• **Courage and strength.** Whatever a hero is, he isn't a coward or quitter. Heroes maintain their composure—and even thrive—under adversity, whether it be the life-threatening sort that war heroes face or the psychological and emotional strains that politicians and business leaders must endure.

• **Honesty.** It's no coincidence that "Honest Abe" Lincoln and George "I cannot tell a lie" Washington are among our nation's most cherished figures. Deceit and deception violate our culture's conception of heroism. "Ronald Reagan once said that Oliver North was an American hero," observes Farley. "But Ollie obviously would founder on the honesty standard."

•**Kind, loving, generous.** Great people may fight fiercely for what they believe, but they are compassionate once the battle is over— toward friend and foe alike. General George S. Patton was a brilliant military man, but his hero status was impaired when he publicly slapped one of his soldiers in the face. "The American public was revolted by that," notes Farley. "He wasn't kind to his men." Though Patton is still regarded as a hero by many, his popularity never recovered.

• **Skill, expertise, intelligence.** So far, our archetypical hero is courageous, kind, honest—in other words, a lot like Forrest Gump. But

Forrest falls short on one measure: A hero's success should stem from his talents and smarts, rather than from mere chance—although, for the sake of modesty, a hero might well attribute his hard-earned achievements to luck.

• **Risk-taking.** "Even though many people won't take risks in their own life, they admire risk-taking in someone else," notes Farley, much of whose research has focused on Type-T personalities—perpetual thrill-seekers. No matter what their calling, heroes are willing to place themselves in some sort of peril. FDR, for example, took enormous political risks by defying the rank and file of his own party; Martin Luther King, Jr., laid his life on the line for his ideals.

• **Objects of affection.** We might be impressed on an intellectual level by somebody's deeds. But admiration is not enough—heroes must win our hearts as well as our minds.

In addition to these six determinants, heroes also exhibit *depth,* the second "D" in Farley's model. Depth is that timeless, mythical, almost otherworldly quality that marks a hero. It's hard to articulate exactly what this is, admits Farley, but we all know it when we see it—it's what makes even physically diminutive heroes seem larger than life.

"I think of depth as sorting out true heroes from celebrities, or the passing hero from the timeless one," Farley says. Clint Eastwood, for example, often shows up on lists of today's heroes because of his rugged individualism. But studies show that he lacks that mythical depth factor that ensures long-standing heroic status.

GREAT EXPECTATIONS

Heroes don't exist in a vacuum. They make specific contributions to the culture. So the third "D" is *domain,* the field in which a hero makes his mark. Although elected officials are currently held in roughly the same regard as, say, carjackers, politics remains the number-one source of heroes. It may help, though, to be a dead politician, or at least a former one: Sitting presidents don't do very well when people are surveyed about their heroes. One reason, Farley thinks, is the intense media scrutiny to which we subject national figures.

Neck and neck for second place among the most common domains of heroes: entertainers (Barbra Streisand is big among women, Clint Eastwood among men) and family members (Mom and Dad, Uncle Bill who lost an arm in the war, your big sister). Religious figures rank fourth, with most of the rest coming from the military, science, sports, and the arts.

Why the low standing of athletes? The sheer number of them, for one; it was much easier for Joe DiMaggio to become a national icon when baseball and football were the only sports of any popularity. Moreover, sports have become big business, with athletes seemingly motivated as much by lucre as by love of the game. Some charge young fans to autograph a baseball. "Would Martin Luther King sell his autograph?" asks Farley, who wonders if public disillusionment with pro athletes means that most of tomorrow's sport heroes will be fictional characters like Rocky.

The fourth "D" is *database,* Farley's term for where we get information about heroes. The main sources are television, radio, magazines. Conspicuous by its absence is the one place where tales of heroism ought to dwell: history class.

"Schools are not dealing enough with studying the lives of people who changed the world and did great things," Farley warns. "Nowadays schools deal more with abstractions, with *isms*—communism, feminism, racism. But if you really want to instruct young people in these ideas, embody them in the life and times of an individual."

The idea of nonviolent protest, for example, must seem quaint or downright irrelevant—to today's kids, who turn on the TV and see the world being changed through violence. "If you talk about nonviolent protest being a viable alternative, they're not going to understand it," Farley explains. "But if you embed it in the life of Gandhi, all of a sudden you see the lights coming on: This little man brought the British Empire to its knees."

WHY WE NEED HEROES

Heroes are more than a convenient way to get kids hooked on history. Above all, they spur us to raise our sights beyond the horizon of the mundane, to attempt the improbable or impossible. "Being inspired by people who do great things is one of the oldest, most reliable forms of motivation," notes Farley. In fact, many heroes themselves, including Winston Churchill and Patton, have cited biography as their favorite form of reading, as a source of both information and inspiration.

In this context, a recent survey reporting that nearly half of kids have no heroes at all has ominous implications. How can our children hope to transcend adversity—such as poverty or racism—without the example of the great men and women who came before them? "The great American story is the person starting from nothing and becoming something," Farley says. "We need more depictions of that."

Heroes are also a window into the soul of a culture. Look at a nation's top heroes, and you'll get a pretty good idea what values its citizens ascribe to, what ideals they cherish. American heroes tend to be individualists and risk-takers. But in China, heroes might be more likely to conserve tradition. That has important implications for everything from international business dealings to political and military negotiations.

HEROES AT HOME

The last "D" is *distance,* how close we are to our heroes. If the mythical quality of many great people makes them seem somewhat distant and inaccessible, that's not true of the answer people most often give when Farley asks them to name their heroes: "Mom" and "Dad."

Parents may not be heroes to the masses. But if their kingdom is small, their influence within that kingdom runs deep indeed. So it's no exaggeration to say that each of us has the potential to be a hero in our way. There are few more effective ways to make a difference than to be a hero.

How Crab Got a Hard Back

retold by Philip Sherlock

Welcome to a world where witches are real and crabs hold conversations. Stories about Anansi, the trickster spider, were brought from West Africa to Jamaica, the source of this tale. You may also be reminded of the European tale of Rumpelstiltskin.

Now in the spring of time, when everything was new, there was an old witch-woman and nobody knew her name. She called herself Old Woman Crim, and though she was very rich she was very mean. She had no children of her own, but she kept animals as her children: Duck, Goat, Crab, and Peacock. These children knew her true name. Crab and Duck knew, and Peacock and Goat, but Old Woman Crim made them promise never to tell. Leaning on a long, crooked stick that she had cut from a tamarind-tree, and holding half a calabash full of magic water, she sprinkled the magic drops over them and said:

> *Water, water, make bad things come,*
> *Who tells my name, I make him dumb,*
> *Water, water, make bad things come,*
> *I make him dumb*
> *I make him dumb.*

So Old Woman Crim's children never told her name.

The witch-woman had a voice that sounded like dry leaves when the wind blows them across the street. A thin, dry voice she had, and bright black eyes like beads, and a long, red purse in which she kept her gold. Old Woman Crim, as she counted her gold, morning and evening, said:

> *I never spent money today,*
> *I made them work right through the day*
> *But I never spent money today.*

This was what Old Woman Crim did. She sent out Parrot, and Kisander the cat, to spread the news that she wanted a girl to work as maid and cook. The girl had to work for a week. At the end of the week, if she guessed Old Woman Crim's true name, she would get half the clothes in the closet, and half the food in the cupboard, and half the gold in the purse.

One girl after another came and worked. Each went away without guessing the name. At the end of the rainy season, a girl from the town came and worked for a week, washing the clothes down by the stream, cooking the food, cleaning the floor, working from day to night with Old Woman Crim saying in her dry, thin voice:

> *Work harder, work harder through the day*
> *Or I'll send you away, send you away.*

At the end of the week the girl went away crying because she could not guess Old Woman Crim's name. The old woman caught the tears in her magical calabash and kept them there.

During the dry season another girl came and worked all week, from sunrise till late at night, and at the end of the week Old Woman Crim said:

> *What's my name? What's my name?*
> *Tell me the same.*

The girl guessed Quasheeba, Selina, Jestina, and all the witch names, but she couldn't guess right. Old Woman Crim sent the girl away hungry, and caught her tears in the magic calabash. So it went on till the witch-woman had the tears of a hundred girls in her calabash. And when it came near to Christmas no more girls came. There were no more girls to clean the house and cook the food and take Old Woman Crim's clothes down to the stream.

93

Try as hard as she could, the old woman could get no more girls. She sent out Parrot far and wide to tell the news. She sent out Kisander the cat to promise half the clothes in the closet, half the food in the cupboard, half the gold in the long, red purse. But no girl came.

Anansi heard Parrot calling the news from tree to tree. He heard Kisander the cat. Anansi wanted some money, for Christmas was coming. He said to himself, "I can find out Old Woman Crim's name. I will dress up as a girl and work for her."

So Anansi dressed himself up as a girl in a pretty white dress with pink spots, and a broad hat, and a little bag, and shoes with pointed toes but not too pointed, for Anansi's feet were large—and high heels but not too high, for Anansi couldn't walk easily in shoes with high heels. Then he set off for Old Woman Crim's home.

The witch-woman was glad when Anansi, dressed as a girl, walked up to the front door and asked for work. She had a lot of clothes ready to be washed. She took on Anansi, and said:

The first thing to do, my daughter—
Go wash these clothes in river water!

Anansi set off with the basket full of clothes and started to wash them in the stream. As he washed, he saw Crab walking along under the shelter of a rock. Anansi thought to himself, "Ah, Crab is Old Woman Crim's child. He knows her name. I will find a way of making him talk."

"Oh, what a pretty gentleman," said Anansi, in a voice like a girl's.

"You like me, girl?" asked Crab. No girl had ever called him a pretty gentleman before. He was very pleased.

"You like me, girl?" he repeated.

"Yes, sir," said Anansi, and smiled at Crab more with her eyes than with her lips, like a girl. "Yes, sir. What a real dandy man, sir! Do you travel far?"

Crab was very happy, hearing how the girl in the white dress with pink spots praised him. He began to boast a little:

"Yes, girl," he said. "I travel all over the world. But you are a nice girl and you have a lot of sense, a lot more sense than any other girl I know. I like you, girl."

"Oh, sir," said Anansi, smiling more than ever, "I like you too. If ever I get into trouble would you help me, sir?"

"Of course," said Crab. "If you ever get into trouble, girl, you come to me and I will help you."

"Thank you, sir, from the bottom of my heart," replied Anansi. "But now I must go. I don't think you will see me again, but I will remember your promise, sir."

"I never break my word," boasted Crab. "But I would like to see you again, girl."

"Perhaps, sir, perhaps," said Anansi as he walked away with the basket of clothes, walking very slowly because he was not quite used to the shoes with pointed toes and high heels.

At the end of the week Anansi was very tired. He had never worked so hard in all his life. Now it was Saturday and Old Mother Crim said to him, "Girl, you have to guess my name. If you guess right you get money and food and clothes. If you guess wrong you get nothing."

Anansi asked for a little time to consider. He went down to the river and sat by the rock where he had seen Crab. He took some of the river water and rubbed his eyes, so that it looked as if he had been crying. The drops trickled down his cheek like tears. He sobbed and whispered, "Poor me girl, poor me girl! What am I to do." He kept on sobbing and whispered, "Poor me girl!"

Crab looked out from his home. He saw the girl in the white dress with pink spots, sobbing. He heard her whispering, "Poor me girl." He went up to her and said:

"Cheer up, girl, what's the matter with you?"

"Sir, I worked for an old lady the whole week and now she won't pay me if I can't guess her name."

"Don't cry, girl," said Crab. "That's Old Woman Crim, my mother. I know her name."

"Oh, poor me girl! Tell me her name, sir. Oh, what am I to do? Christmas coming and no money! Help me, sir."

"Very well, girl," said Crab. "I promised to help you and I will." Crab whispered the name in Anansi's ear.

Anansi never even waited to say thanks. He ran up the bank of the stream without stopping to pick up the high-heeled shoes when they fell off. He ran to Old Woman Crim's home so fast that he was out of breath when he got there. The witch-woman shrieked, "Girl, can you guess my name?"

"I am not sure, ma'am," replied Anansi.

"Guess," screamed Old Woman Crim. "Guess three times. Guess my name and you get the gold. Guess wrong and off you go."

"Your name is Mother Jane," cried Anansi.

"Wrong, wrong, first time wrong."

Anansi said slowly, "Your name is Mother Jonkanoo."

"Wrong, wrong, second time wrong."

"Guess again, then get along," cried the old witch-woman, and now her voice was like the crackling of fire in dry bush. She held her purse tight, for she was sure she would not have to pay out any money. She shrieked:

"Guess again, then get along!"

"Your name is Mother Cantinny," cried Anansi. "Mother Cantinny, Mother Cantinny." Anansi shouted the name aloud so that Parrot heard it and Kisander the cat also. Old Woman Crim fell to the ground as if she were dead. Then she got up, and gave Anansi half the clothes in the closet, half the food in the cupboard, half the gold in the long, red purse. As he went off through the gate, Anansi said, "Anansi guessed your name, Old Woman Crim, old Mother Cantinny!"

Mother Cantinny was very angry. "Anansi must have worked a trick on one of my children," she said to herself. She called together Duck, Goat, Peacock, and Crab and stood them in a line. Then she said:

> *They say that I am Cantinny,*
> *They call me Old Crim,*
> *I am Crim, you are Crim*
> *And Cantinny,*
> *Who said Cantinny?*
> *Who said Cantinny?*

She looked into the face of each one as she asked, "Who said Cantinny?"

She stared at Goat, and Goat stared back at her.

She stared at Duck, and Duck stared back at her.

She stared at Peacock, and Peacock stared back at her.

She stared at Crab, and Crab held his face down, looking at the ground.

"It's you, it's you," she cried. She threw the magic calabash at him. Crab turned and ran, but the calabash fell on his back, and the tears of all the girls held it fast. There it is. That is how Crab got his hard back. Anansi made it happen.

Problems with Hurricanes

by Victor Hernández Cruz

A campesino looked at the air
and told me:

With hurricanes it's not the wind
or the noise or the water.
I'll tell you he said:
it's the mangoes, avocados
Green plantains and bananas
flying into town like projectiles.

How would your family
feel if they had to tell
The generations that you
got killed by a flying
Banana.

Death by drowning has honor
If the wind picked you up
and slammed you
Against a mountain boulder
This would not carry shame
But
to suffer a mango smashing
Your skull
or a plantain hitting your
Temple at 70 miles per hour
is the ultimate disgrace.

The campesino takes off his hat—
As a sign of respect
towards the fury of the wind
And says:
Don't worry about the noise
Don't worry about the water
Don't worry about the wind—

If you are going out
beware of mangoes
And all such beautiful
sweet things.

97

The Possibility of Evil

by Shirley Jackson

You don't need weird monsters and exotic settings for a story about cruelty and strange events. Those can spring up among nice people ... or in the house next door.

Miss Adela Strangeworth stepped daintily along Main Street on her way to the grocery. The sun was shining, the air was fresh and clear after the night's heavy rain, and everything in Miss Strangeworth's little town looked washed and bright. Miss Strangeworth took deep breaths, and thought that there was nothing in the world like a fragrant summer day.

She knew everyone in town, of course; she was fond of telling strangers—tourists who sometimes passed through the town and stopped to admire Miss Strangeworth's roses—that she had never spent more than a day outside this town in all her long life. She was seventy-one, Miss Strangeworth told the tourists, with a pretty little dimple showing by her lip, and she sometimes found herself thinking that the town belonged to her. "My grandfather built the first house on Pleasant Street," she would say, opening her blue eyes wide with the wonder of it. "This house, right here. My family has lived here for better than a hundred years. My grandmother planted these roses, and my mother tended them, just as I do. I've watched my town grow; I can remember when Mr. Lewis, Senior, opened the grocery store, and the year the river flooded out the shanties on the low road, and the excitement when some young folks wanted to move the park over to the space in front of where the new post office is today. They wanted to put up a statue of Ethan Allen"—Miss Strangeworth would frown a little and sound stern—"but it should have been a statue of my grandfather. There wouldn't have been a town here at all if it hadn't been for my grandfather and the lumber mill."

Miss Strangeworth never gave away any of her roses although the tourists often asked her. The roses belonged on Pleasant Street, and it bothered Miss Strangeworth to think of people wanting to carry them away, to take them into strange towns and down strange streets. When the new minister came, and the ladies were gathering flowers to decorate the church, Miss Strangeworth sent over a great basket of gladioli; when she picked the roses at all, she set them in bowls and vases around the inside of the house her grandfather had built.

Walking down Main Street on a summer morning, Miss Strangeworth had to stop every minute or so to say good morning to someone or to ask after someone's health. When she came into the grocery, half a dozen people turned away from the shelves and the counters to wave at her or call out good morning.

"And good morning to you, too, Mr. Lewis," Miss Strangeworth said at last. The Lewis family had been in the town almost as long as the Strangeworths; but the day young Lewis left high school and went to work in the grocery, Miss Strangeworth had stopped calling him Tommy and started calling him Mr. Lewis, and he had stopped calling her Addie and started calling her Miss Strangeworth. They had been in high school together, and had gone to picnics together, and to high school dances and basketball games; but now Mr. Lewis was behind the counter in the grocery, and Miss Strangeworth was living alone in the Strangeworth house on Pleasant Street.

"Good morning," Mr. Lewis said, and added politely, "lovely day."

"It is a very nice day," Miss Strangeworth said as though she had only just decided that it would do after all. "I would like a chop, please, Mr. Lewis, a small, lean veal chop. Are those strawberries from

Arthur Parker's garden? They're early this year."

"He brought them in this morning," Mr. Lewis said.

"I shall have a box," Miss Strangeworth said. Mr. Lewis looked worried, she thought, and for a minute she hesitated, but then she decided that he surely could not be worried over the strawberries. He looked very tired indeed. He was usually so chipper, Miss Strangeworth thought, and almost commented, but it was far too personal a subject to be introduced to Mr. Lewis, the grocer, so she only said, "And a can of cat food and, I think, a tomato."

Silently, Mr. Lewis assembled her order on the counter and waited. Miss Strangeworth looked at him curiously and then said, "It's Tuesday, Mr. Lewis. You forgot to remind me."

"Did I? Sorry."

"Imagine your forgetting that I always buy my tea on Tuesday," Miss Strangeworth said gently. "A quarter pound of tea, please, Mr. Lewis."

"Is that all, Miss Strangeworth?"

"Yes, thank you, Mr. Lewis. Such a lovely day, isn't it?"

"Lovely," Mr. Lewis said.

Miss Strangeworth moved slightly to make room for Mrs. Harper at the counter. "Morning, Adela," Mrs. Harper said, and Miss Strangeworth said, "Good morning, Martha."

"Lovely day," Mrs. Harper said, and Miss Strangeworth said, "Yes, lovely," and Mr. Lewis, under Mrs. Harper's glance, nodded.

"Ran out of sugar for my cake frosting," Mrs. Harper explained. Her hand shook slightly as she opened her pocketbook. Miss Strangeworth wondered, glancing at her quickly, if she had been taking proper care of herself. Martha Harper was not as young as she used to be, Miss Strangeworth thought. She probably could use a good, strong tonic.

"Martha," she said, "you don't look well."

"I'm perfectly all right," Mrs. Harper said shortly. She handed her money to Mr. Lewis, took her change and her sugar, and went out without speaking again. Looking after her, Miss Strangeworth shook her head slightly. Martha definitely did *not* look well.

Carrying her little bag of groceries, Miss Strangeworth came out of the store into the bright sunlight and stopped to smile down on the Crane baby. Don and Helen Crane were really the two most infatuated young parents she had ever known, she thought indulgently, looking at the delicately embroidered baby cap and the lace-edged carriage cover.

"That little girl is going to grow up expecting luxury all her life," she said to Helen Crane.

Helen laughed. "That's the way we want her to feel," she said. "Like a princess."

"A princess can be a lot of trouble sometimes," Miss Strangeworth said dryly. "How old is her highness now?"

"Six months next Tuesday," Helen Crane said, looking down with rapt wonder at her child. "I've been worrying, though, about her. Don't you think she ought to move around more? Try to sit up, for instance?"

"For plain and fancy worrying," Miss Strangeworth said, amused, "give me a new mother every time."

"She just seems—slow," Helen Crane said.

"Nonsense. All babies are different. Some of them develop much more quickly than others."

"That's what my mother says." Helen Crane laughed, looking a little bit ashamed.

"I suppose you've got young Don all upset about the fact that his daughter is already six months old and hasn't yet begun to learn to dance?"

"I haven't mentioned it to him. I suppose she's just so precious that I worry about her all the time."

"Well, apologize to her right now," Miss Strangeworth said. "*She* is probably worrying about why you keep jumping around all the time." Smiling to herself and shaking her old head, she went on down the sunny street, stopping once to ask little Billy Moore why he wasn't out riding in his daddy's shiny new car, and talking for a few minutes outside the library with Miss Chandler, the librarian, about the new novels to be ordered, and paid for by the annual library appropriation. Miss Chandler seemed absentminded and very much as though she was thinking about something else. Miss Strangeworth noticed that Miss Chandler had not taken much trouble with her hair that morning, and sighed. Miss Strangeworth hated sloppiness.

Many people seemed disturbed recently, Miss Strangeworth thought. Only yesterday the Stewarts' fifteen-year-old Linda had run crying down her own front walk and all the way to school, not caring who saw her. People around town thought she might have had a fight with the Harris boy, but they showed up together at the soda shop after school as usual, both of them looking grim and bleak. Trouble at home, people concluded, and sighed over the problems of trying to raise kids right these days.

From halfway down the block Miss Strangeworth could catch the heavy accent of her roses, and she moved a little more quickly. The perfume of roses meant home, and home meant the Strangeworth House on Pleasant Street. Miss Strangeworth stopped at her own front gate, as she always did, and looked with deep pleasure at her house, with the red and pink and white roses massed along the narrow lawn, and the rambler going up along the porch; and the neat, the unbelievably trim lines of the house itself, with its slimness and its washed white look. Every window sparkled, every curtain hung stiff and straight, and even the stones of the front walk were swept and clear. People around town wondered how old Miss Strangeworth managed to keep the house looking the way it did, and there was a legend about a tourist once mistaking it for the local museum and going all through the place without finding out about his mistake. But the town was proud of Miss Strangeworth and her roses and her house. They had all grown together. Miss Strangeworth went up her front steps, unlocked her front door with her key, and went into the kitchen to put away her groceries. She debated having a cup of tea and then decided that it was too close to midday dinnertime; she would not have the appetite for her little chop if she had tea now. Instead she went into the light, lovely sitting room, which still glowed from the hands of her mother and her grandmother, who had covered the chairs with bright chintz and hung the curtains. All the furniture was spare and shining, and the round hooked rugs on the floor had been the work of Miss Strangeworth's grandmother and her mother. Miss Strangeworth had put a bowl of her red roses on the low table before the window, and the room was full of their scent.

Miss Strangeworth went to the narrow desk in the corner, and unlocked it with her key. She never knew when she might feel like writing letters, so she kept her notepaper inside, and the desk locked. Miss Strangeworth's usual stationery was heavy and cream-colored, with "Strangeworth House" engraved across the top, but, when she felt like writing her other letters, Miss Strangeworth used a pad of various-colored paper, bought from the local newspaper shop. It was almost a town joke, that colored paper, layered in pink and green and blue and yellow; everyone in town bought it and used it for odd, informal notes and shopping lists. It was usual to remark, upon receiving a note written on a blue page, that so-and-so would be needing a new pad soon—here she was, down to the blue already. Everyone used the matching envelopes for tucking away recipes, or keeping odd little things in, or even to hold cookies in the school lunch boxes. Mr. Lewis sometimes gave them to the children for carrying home penny candy.

Although Miss Strangeworth's desk held a trimmed quill pen, which had belonged to her grandfather, and a gold-frost fountain pen, which had belonged to her father, Miss Strangeworth always used a dull stub of pencil when she wrote her letters, and she printed them in a childish block print. After thinking for a minute, although she had been phrasing the letter in the back of her mind all the way home, she wrote on a pink sheet: *Didn't you ever see an idiot child before? Some people just shouldn't have children, should they?*

She was pleased with the letter. She was fond of doing things exactly right. When she made a mistake, as she sometimes did, or when the letters were not spaced nicely on the page, she had to take the discarded page to the kitchen stove and burn it at once. Miss Strangeworth never delayed when things had to be done.

After thinking for a minute, she decided that she would like to write another letter, perhaps to go to Mrs. Harper, to follow up the ones she had already mailed. She selected a green sheet this time and wrote quickly: *Have you found out yet what they were all laughing about after you left the bridge club on Thursday? Or is the wife really always the last one to know?*

Miss Strangeworth never concerned herself with facts; her letters all dealt with the more negotiable stuff of suspicion. Mr. Lewis would never have imagined for a minute that his grandson might be lifting petty cash from the store register if he had not had one of Miss Strangeworth's letters. Miss Chandler, the librarian, and Linda Stewart's parents would have gone unsuspectingly ahead with their lives, never aware of possible evil lurking nearby, if Miss Strangeworth had not sent letters to open their eyes. Miss Strangeworth would have been genuinely shocked if there *had* been anything between Linda Stewart and the Harris boy, but, as long as evil existed unchecked in the world, it was Miss Strangeworth's duty to keep her town alert to it. It was far more sensible for Miss Chandler to wonder what Mr. Shelley's first wife had really died of than to take a chance on not knowing. There were so many wicked people in the world and only one Strangeworth left in town. Besides, Miss Strangeworth liked writing her letters.

She addressed an envelope to Don Crane after a moment's thought, wondering curiously if he would show the letter to his wife, and using a pink envelope to match the pink paper. Then she addressed a second envelope, green, to Mrs. Harper. Then an idea came to her and she selected a blue sheet and wrote: *You never know about doctors. Remember they're only human and need money like the rest of us. Suppose the knife slipped accidentally. Would Doctor Burns get his fee and a little extra from that nephew of yours?*

She addressed the blue envelope to old Mrs. Foster, who was having an operation next month. She had thought of writing one more letter, to the head of the school board, asking how a chemistry teacher like Billy Moore's father could afford a new convertible, but all at once she was tired of writing letters. The three she had done would do for one day. She could write more tomorrow; it was not as though they all had to be done at once.

She had been writing her letters—sometimes two or three every day for a week, sometimes no more than one in a month—for the past year. She never got any answers, of course, because she never signed her name. If she had been asked, she would have said that her name, Adela Strangeworth, a name honored in the town for so many years, did not belong on such trash. The town where she lived had to be kept clean and sweet, but people everywhere were lustful and evil and degraded, and needed to be watched; the world was so large, and there was only one Strangeworth left in it. Miss Strangeworth sighed, locked her desk, and put the letters into her big, black leather pocketbook, to be mailed when she took her evening walk.

She broiled her little chop nicely, and had a sliced tomato and good cup of tea ready when she sat down to her midday dinner at the table in her dining room, which could be opened to seat twenty-two, with a second table, if necessary, in the hall. Sitting in the warm sunlight that came through the tall windows of the dining room, seeing her roses massed outside, handling the heavy, old silverware and the fine, translucent china, Miss Strangeworth was pleased; she would not have cared to be doing anything else. People must live graciously, after all, she thought, and sipped her tea. Afterward, when her plate and cup and saucer were washed and dried and put back onto the shelves where they belonged, and her silverware was back in the mahogany silver chest, Miss Strangeworth went up the graceful staircase and into her bedroom, which was the front room overlooking the roses, and had been her mother's and her grandmother's. Their Crown Derby dresser set and furs had been kept here, their fans and silver-backed brushes and their own bowls of roses; Miss Strangeworth kept a bowl of white roses on the bed table.

She drew the shades, took the rose-satin spread from the bed, slipped out of her dress and her shoes, and lay down tiredly. She knew that no doorbell or phone would ring; no one in town would dare to disturb Miss Strangeworth during her afternoon nap. She slept, deep in the rich smell of roses.

After her nap she worked in her garden for a little while, sparing herself because of the heat; then she went in to her supper. She ate asparagus from her own garden, with sweet-butter sauce, and a soft-boiled egg, and, while she had her supper, she listened to a late-evening news broadcast and then to a program of classical music on her small radio. After her dishes were done and her kitchen set in order, she took up her hat—Miss Strangeworth's hats were proverbial in the town; people believed that she had inherited them from her mother and her grandmother—and, locking the front door of her house behind her, set off on her evening walk, pocketbook under her arm. She nodded to Linda Stewart's father, who was washing his car in the pleasantly cool evening. She thought that he looked troubled.

There was only one place in town where she could mail her letters, and that was the new post office, shiny with red brick and silver letters. Although Miss Strangeworth had never given the matter any particular thought, she had always made a point of mailing her letters very secretly; it would, of course, not have been wise to let anyone see her mail them. Consequently, she timed her walk so she could reach the post office just as darkness was starting to dim the outlines of the trees and the shapes of people's faces, although no one could ever mistake Miss Strangeworth, with her dainty walk and her rustling skirts.

There was always a group of young people around the post office, the very youngest roller-skating upon its driveway, which went all the way around the building and was the only smooth road in town; and the slightly older ones already knowing how to gather in small groups and chatter and laugh and make great, excited plans for going across the street to the soda shop in a minute or two. Miss Strangeworth had never had any self-consciousness before the children. She did not feel that any of them were staring at her unduly or longing to laugh at her; it would have been most reprehensible for their parents to permit their children to mock Miss Strangeworth of Pleasant Street. Most of the children stood back respectfully as Miss Strangeworth passed, silenced briefly in her presence, and some of the older children greeted her, saying soberly, "Hello, Miss Strangeworth."

Miss Strangeworth smiled at them and quickly went on. It had been a long time since she had known the name of every child in town. The mail slot was in the door of the post office. The children stood away as Miss Strangeworth approached it, seemingly surprised that anyone should want to use the post office after it had been officially closed up for the night and turned over to the children. Miss Strangeworth stood by the door, opening her black pocketbook to take out the letters, and heard a voice which she knew at once to be Linda Stewart's. Poor little Linda was crying again, and Miss Strangeworth listened carefully. This was, after all, her town, and these were her people; if one of them was in trouble, she ought to know about it.

"I can't tell you, Dave," Linda was saying—so she *was* talking to the Harris boy, as Miss Strangeworth had supposed— "I just *can't*. It's just *nasty*."

"But why won't your father let me come around anymore? What on earth did I do?"

"I can't tell you. I just wouldn't tell you for *any*thing. You've got to have a dirty dirty mind for things like that."

"But something's happened. You've been crying and crying, and your father is all upset. Why can't *I* know about it, too? Aren't I like one of the family?"

"Not anymore, Dave, not anymore. You're not to come near our house again; my father said so. He said he'd horsewhip you. That's all I can tell you: You're not to come near our house anymore."

"But I didn't *do* anything."

"Just the same, my father said . . ."

Miss Strangeworth sighed and turned away. There was so much evil in people. Even in a charming little town like this one, there was still so much evil in people.

She slipped her letters into the slot, and two of them fell inside. The third caught on the edge and fell outside, onto the ground at Miss Strangeworth's feet. She did not notice it because she was wondering whether a letter to the Harris boy's father might not be of some service in wiping out this potential badness. Wearily Miss Strangeworth turned to go home to her quiet bed in her lovely house, and never heard the Harris boy calling to her to say that she had dropped something.

"Old lady Strangeworth's getting deaf," he said, looking after her and holding in his hand the letter he had picked up.

"Well, who cares?" Linda said. "Who cares anymore, anyway?"

"It's for Don Crane," the Harris boy said, "this letter. She dropped a letter addressed to Don Crane. Might as well take it on over. We pass his house anyway." He laughed. "Maybe it's got a check or something in it and he'd be just as glad to get it tonight instead of tomorrow."

"Catch old lady Strangeworth sending anybody a check," Linda said. "Throw it in the post office. Why do anyone a favor?" She sniffed. "Doesn't seem to me anybody around here cares about us," she said. "Why should we care about them?"

"I'll take it over, anyway," the Harris boy said. "Maybe it's good news for them. Maybe they need something happy tonight, too. Like us."

Sadly, holding hands, they wandered off down the dark street, the Harris boy carrying Miss Strangeworth's pink envelope in his hand.

Miss Strangeworth awakened the next morning with a feeling of intense happiness and, for a minute, wondered why, and then remembered that this morning three people would open her letters. Harsh, perhaps, at first, but wickedness was never easily banished, and a clean heart was a scoured heart. She washed her soft, old face and brushed her teeth, still sound in spite of her seventy-one years, and dressed herself carefully in her sweet, soft clothes and buttoned shoes. Then, going downstairs, reflecting that perhaps a little waffle would be agreeable for breakfast in the sunny dining room, she found the mail on the hall floor, and bent to pick it up. A bill, the morning paper, a letter in a green envelope that looked oddly familiar. Miss Strangeworth stood perfectly still for a minute, looking down at the green envelope with the penciled printing, and thought: It looks like one of my letters. Was one of my letters sent back? No, because no one would know where to send it. How did this get here?

Miss Strangeworth was a Strangeworth of Pleasant Street. Her hand did not shake as she opened the envelope and unfolded the sheet of green paper inside. She began to cry silently for the wickedness of the world when she read the words: *Look out at what used to be your roses.*

Ghosts

by Sandra Gardner

On Sunday mornings, my father and my uncle,
both widowed, in their 70's and feeling their age,
would sit together for hours, over coffee and bagels
and the Sunday papers, in the sunny room
that had been my aunt's sewing room.

They talked of their children, their children's
children, their youth, past scandals,
cold winters, getting old.

Sometimes they sat silent, thinking of the one
who had bound them together, made them put aside
differences, made them become friends
for her sake, the sister, the wife.

They sat silent, her ghost between them,
never saying her name aloud, pushing away
the angel of death, refusing to give her up.

My uncle died in his sleep
one cold black night last winter.
Now my father sits alone with two ghosts,
hugging them tight to him,
never saying their names.

The 11:59

by Patricia C. McKissack

*The main purpose of a ghost story is to scare the
reader. The story doesn't need to include a logical
explanation of its strange events. This is a classic tale
about the phantom train that stops for all of us, sooner
or later.*

Lester Simmons was a thirty-year retired Pullman car porter—had
his gold watch to prove it. "Keeps perfect train time," he often
bragged. "Good to the second."

Daily he went down to the St. Louis Union Station and shined shoes
to help supplement his meager twenty-four-dollar-a-month Pullman
retirement check. He ate his evening meal at the porter house on
Compton Avenue and hung around until late at night talking union,
playing bid whist, and spinning yarns with those who were still
"travelin' men." In this way Lester stayed in touch with the only family
he'd known since 1920.

There was nothing the young porters liked more than listening to
Lester tell true stories about the old days, during the founding of the
Brotherhood of Sleeping Car Porters, the first black union in the United
States. He knew the president, A. Philip Randolph, personally, and

110

proudly boasted that it was Randolph who'd signed him up as a union man back in 1926. He passed his original card around for inspection. "I knew all the founding brothers. Take Brother E. J. Bradley. We hunted many a day together, not for the sport of it but for something to eat. Those were hard times, starting up the union. But we hung in there so you youngsters might have the benefits you enjoy now."

The rookie porters always liked hearing about the thirteen-year struggle between the Brotherhood and the powerful Pullman Company, and how, against all odds, the fledgling union had won recognition and better working conditions.

Everybody enjoyed it too when Lester told tall tales about Daddy Joe, the porters' larger-than-life hero. "Now y'all know the first thing a good Pullman man is expected to do is make up the top and lower berths for the passengers each night."

"Come on, Lester," one of his listeners chided. "You don't need to describe our jobs for us."

"Some of you, maybe not. But some of you, well—" he said, looking over the top of his glasses and raising an eyebrow at a few of the younger porters. "I was just setting the stage." He smiled good-naturedly and went on with his story. "They tell me Daddy Joe could walk flatfooted down the center of the coach and let down berths on both sides of the aisle."

Hearty laughter filled the room, because everyone knew that to accomplish such a feat, Daddy Joe would have to have been super-human. But that was it: To the men who worked the sleeping cars, Daddy Joe was no less a hero than Paul Bunyan was to the lumberjacks of the Northwestern forests.

"And when the 11:59 pulled up to his door, as big and strong as Daddy Joe was . . ." Lester continued solemnly. "Well, in the end even he couldn't escape the 11:59." The old storyteller eyed one of the rookie porters he knew had never heard the frightening tale about the porters' Death Train. Lester took joy in mesmerizing his young listeners with all the details.

"Any porter who hears the whistle of the 11:59 has got exactly twenty-four hours to clear up earthly matters. He better be ready when the train comes the next night . . ." In his creakiest voice, Lester drove home the point. "All us porters got to board that train one day. Ain't no way to escape the final ride on the 11:59."

Silence.

"Lester," a young porter asked, "you know anybody who ever heard the whistle of the 11:59 and lived to tell—"

"Not a living soul!"

Laughter.

"Well," began one of the men, "wonder will we have to make up berths on *that* train?"

"If it's an overnight trip to heaven, you can best be believing there's bound to be a few of us making up the berths," another answered.

"Shucks," a card player stopped to put in. "They say even up in heaven *we* the ones gon' be keeping all that gold and silver polished."

"Speaking of gold and silver," Lester said, remembering. "That reminds me of how I gave Tip Sampson his nickname. Y'all know Tip?"

There were plenty of nods and smiles.

The memory made Lester chuckle. He shifted in his seat to find a more comfortable spot. Then he began. "A woman got on board the *Silver Arrow* in Chicago going to Los Angeles. She was dripping in finery—had on all kinds of gold and diamond jewelry, carried twelve bags. Sampson knocked me down getting to wait on her, figuring she was sure for a big tip. That lady was worrisome! Ooo-wee! 'Come do this. Go do that. Bring me this.' Sampson was running over himself trying to keep that lady happy. When we reached L.A., my passengers all tipped me two or three dollars, as was customary back then.

"When Sampson's Big Money lady got off, she reached into her purse and placed a dime in his outstretched hand. A *dime!* Can you imagine? *Ow!* You should have seen his face. And I didn't make it no better. Never did let him forget it. I teased him so—went to calling him Tip, and the nickname stuck."

Laughter.

"I haven't heard from ol' Tip in a while. Anybody know anything?"

"You haven't got word, Lester? Tip boarded the 11:59 over in Kansas City about a month ago."

"Sorry to hear that. That just leaves me and Willie Beavers, the last of the old, old-timers here in St. Louis."

Lester looked at his watch—it was a little before midnight. The talkfest had lasted later than usual. He said his good-byes and left, taking his usual route across the Eighteenth Street bridge behind the station.

In the darkness, Lester looked over the yard, picking out familiar shapes—the *Hummingbird,* the *Zephyr.* He'd worked on them both. Train travel wasn't anything like it used to be in the old days—not since people had begun to ride airplanes. "Progress," he scoffed. "Those contraptions will never take the place of a train. No sir!"

Suddenly he felt a sharp pain in his chest. At exactly the same moment he heard the mournful sound of a train whistle, which the wind seemed to carry from some faraway place. Ignoring his pain, Lester looked at the old station. He knew nothing was scheduled to come in or out till early morning. Nervously he lit a match to check the time. 11:59!

"No," he said into the darkness. "I'm not ready. I've got plenty of living yet."

Fear quickened his step. Reaching his small apartment, he hurried up the steps. His heart pounded in his ear, and his left arm tingled. He had an idea, and there wasn't a moment to waste. But his own words haunted him. *Ain't no way to escape the final ride on the 11:59.*

"But I'm gon' try!" Lester spent the rest of the night plotting his escape from fate.

"I won't eat or drink anything all day," he talked himself through his plan. "That way I can't choke, die of food poisoning, or cause a cooking fire."

Lester shut off the space heater to avoid an explosion, nailed shut all doors and windows to keep out intruders, and unplugged every electrical appliance. Good weather was predicted, but just in case a freak storm came and blew out a window, shooting deadly glass shards in his direction, he moved a straight-backed chair into a far corner, making sure nothing was overhead to fall on him.

"I'll survive," he said, smiling at the prospect of beating Death. "Won't that be a wonderful story to tell at the porter house?" He rubbed his left arm. It felt numb again.

Lester sat silently in his chair all day, too afraid to move. At noon someone knocked on his door. He couldn't answer it. Footsteps . . . another knock. He didn't answer.

A parade of minutes passed by, equally measured, one behind the other, ticking . . . ticking . . . away . . . The dull pain in his chest returned. He nervously checked his watch every few minutes.

Ticktock, ticktock.

Time had always been on his side. Now it was his enemy. Where had the years gone? Lester reviewed the thirty years he'd spent riding the rails. How different would his life have been if he'd married Louise Henderson and had a gallon of children? What if he'd taken that job at the mill down in Opelika? What if he'd followed his brother to Philly? How different?

Ticktock, ticktock.

So much living had passed so quickly. Lester decided if he had to do it all over again, he'd stand by his choices. His had been a good life. No regrets. No major changes for him.

Ticktock, ticktock.

The times he'd had—both good and bad—what memories. His first and only love had been traveling, and she was a jealous companion. Wonder whatever happened to that girl up in Minneapolis? Thinking about her made him smile. Then he laughed. That *girl* must be close to seventy years old by now.

Ticktock, ticktock.

Daylight was fading quickly. Lester drifted off to sleep, then woke from a nightmare in which, like Jonah, he'd been swallowed by an enormous beast. Even awake he could still hear its heart beating ... *ticktock, ticktock* ... But then he realized he was hearing his own heartbeat.

Lester couldn't see his watch, but he guessed no more than half an hour had passed. Sleep had overtaken him with such little resistance. Would Death, that shapeless shadow, slip in that easily? Where was he lurking? *Yea, though I walk through the valley of the shadow of death, I will fear no evil* ...The Twenty-third Psalm was the only prayer Lester knew, and he repeated it over and over, hoping it would comfort him.

Lester rubbed his tingling arm. He could hear the blood rushing past his ear and up the side of his head. He longed to know what time it was, but that meant he had to light a match—too risky. What if there was a gas leak? The match would set off an explosion. "I'm too smart for that, Death," he said.

Ticktock, ticktock.

It was late. He could feel it. Stiffness seized his legs and made them tremble. How much longer? he wondered. Was he close to winning?

Then in the fearful silence he heard a train whistle. His ears strained to identify the sound, making sure it *was* a whistle. No mistake. It came again, the same as the night before. Lester answered it with a groan.

Ticktock, ticktock.

He could hear Time ticking away in his head. Gas leak or not, he had to see his watch. Striking a match, Lester quickly checked the time. 11:57.

Although there was no gas explosion, a tiny explosion erupted in his heart.

Ticktock, ticktock.

Just a little more time. The whistle sounded again. Closer than before. Lester struggled to move, but he felt fastened to the chair. Now he could hear the engine puffing, pulling a heavy load. It was hard for him to breathe, too, and the pain in his chest weighed heavier and heavier.

Ticktock, ticktock.

Time had run out! Lester's mind reached for an explanation that made sense. But reason failed when a glowing phantom dressed in the porters' blue uniform stepped out of the grayness of Lester's confusion.

"It's *your* time, good brother." The specter spoke in a thousand familiar voices.

Freed of any restraint now, Lester stood, bathed in a peaceful calm that had its own glow. "Is that you, Tip?" he asked, squinting to focus on his old friend standing in the strange light.

"It's me, ol' partner. Come to remind you that none of us can escape the last ride on the 11:59."

"I know. I know," Lester said, chuckling. "But man, I had to try."

Tip smiled. "I can dig it. So did I."

"That'll just leave Willie, won't it?"

"Not for long."

"I'm ready."

Lester saw the great beam of the single headlight and heard the deafening whistle blast one last time before the engine tore through the front of the apartment, shattering glass and splintering wood, collapsing everything in its path, including Lester's heart.

When Lester didn't show up at the shoeshine stand two days running, friends went over to his place and found him on the floor. His eyes were fixed on something quite amazing—his gold watch, stopped at exactly 11:59.

The Others

by Joyce Carol Oates

The curtain that separates the living from the dead lifts for one man, in this evocative story by a renowned writer.

Early one evening in a crowd of people, most of them commuters, he happened to see, quite by accident—he'd taken a slightly different route that day, having left the building in which he worked by an entrance he rarely used—and this, as he'd recall afterward, with the fussy precision which had characterized him since childhood, and helped to account for his success in his profession, because there was renovation being done in the main lobby—a man he had not seen in years, or was it decades: a face teasingly familiar, yet made strange by time, like an old photograph about to disintegrate into its elements.

Spence followed the man into the street, into blowsy damp dusk, but did not catch up to him and introduce himself: that wasn't his way. He was certain he knew the man, and that the man knew him, but how, or why, or from what period in his life the man dated, he could not have said. Spence was forty-two years old and the other seemed to be about that age, yet, oddly, older: his skin liverish, his profile vague as if seen through an element transparent yet dense, like water; his clothing—handsome tweed overcoat, sharply creased gray trousers—hanging slack on him, as if several sizes too large.

Outside, Spence soon lost sight of the man in a swarm of pedestrians crossing the street; and made no effort to locate him again. But for most of the ride home on the train he thought of nothing else: who was that man, why was he certain the man would have known him, what were they to each other, resembling each other only very slightly, yet close as twins? He felt stabs of excitement that left him weak and breathless but it wasn't until that night, when he and his wife were undressing for bed, that he said, or heard himself say in a voice of bemused wonder, and dread: "I saw someone today who looked just like my cousin Sandy—"

"Did I know Sandy?" his wife asked.

"—my cousin Sandy who died, who drowned, when we were both in college."

"But did I know him?" his wife asked. She cast him an impatient sidelong glance and smiled her sweet-derisive smile. "It's difficult to envision him if I've never seen him, and if he's been dead for so long, why should it matter so much to you?"

Spence had begun to perspire. His heart beat hard and steady as if in the presence of danger. "I don't understand what you're saying," he said.

"The actual words, or their meaning?"

"The words."

She laughed as if he had said something witty, and did not answer him. As he fell asleep he tried not to think of his cousin Sandy whom he had not seen in twenty years and whom he'd last seen in an open casket in a funeral home in Damascus, Minnesota.

The second episode occurred a few weeks later when Spence was in line at a post office, not the post office he usually frequented but another, larger, busier, in a suburban township adjacent to his own, and the elderly woman in front of him drew his attention: wasn't she, too, someone he knew? or had known, many years ago? He stared, fascinated, at her stitched-looking skin, soft and puckered as a glove of some exquisite material, and unnaturally white; her eyes that were small, sunken, yet shining; her astonishing hands—delicate, even skeletal, discolored by liver spots like coins, yet with rings on several fingers, and in a way rather beautiful. The woman appeared to be in her mid-nineties, if not older: fussy, anxious, very possibly addled: complaining ceaselessly to herself, or to others by way of herself. Yet her manner was mirthful; nervous bustling energy crackled about her like invisible bees.

He believed he knew who she was: Miss Reuter, a teacher of his in elementary school. Whom he had not seen in more years than he wanted to calculate.

Miss Reuter, though enormously aged, was able, it seemed, to get around by herself. She carried a large rather glitzy shopping bag made of a silvery material, and in this bag, and in another at her feet, she was rummaging for her change purse, as she called it, which she could not seem to find. The post-office clerk waited with a show of strained patience; the line now consisted of a half-dozen people.

Spence asked Miss Reuter—for surely it was she: while virtually unrecognizable she was at the same time unmistakable—if she needed some assistance. He did not call her by name and as she turned to him, in exasperation, and gratitude—as if she knew that he, or someone, would come shortly to her aid—she did not seem to recognize him. Spence paid for her postage and a roll of stamps, and Miss Reuter, still rummaging in her bag, vexed, cheerful, befuddled, thanked him without looking up at him. She insisted it must be a loan, and not a gift, for she was, she said, "not yet an object of public charity."

Afterward Spence put the incident out of his mind, knowing the woman was dead. It was purposeless to think of it, and would only upset him.

After that he began to see them more frequently. The Others—as he thought of them. On the street, in restaurants, at church; in the building in which he worked; on the very floor, in the very department, in which his office was located. (He was a tax lawyer for one of the largest of American "conglomerates"—yes and very well paid.) One morning his wife saw him standing at a bedroom window looking out toward the street. She poked him playfully in the ribs. "What's wrong?" she said. "None of this behavior suits you."

"There's someone out there, at the curb."

"No one's there."

"I have the idea he's waiting for me."

"Oh yes, I do see someone," his wife said carelessly. "He's often there. But I doubt that he's waiting for you."

She laughed, as at a private joke. She was a pretty freckled snub-nosed woman given to moments of mysterious amusement. Spence had married her long ago in a trance of love from which he had yet to awaken.

Spence said, his voice shaking, "I think—I'm afraid I think I might be having a nervous breakdown. I'm so very, very afraid."

"No," said his wife, "—you're the sanest person I know. All surface and no cracks, fissures, potholes."

Spence turned to her. His eyes were filling with tears.

"Don't joke. Have pity."

She made no reply; seemed about to drift away; then slipped an arm around his waist and nudged her head against his shoulder in a gesture of camaraderie. Whether mocking, or altogether genuine, Spence could not have said.

"It's just that I'm so afraid."

"Yes, you've said."

"—of losing my mind. Going mad."

She stood for a moment, peering out toward the street. The elderly gentleman standing at the curb glanced back but could not have seen them, or anyone, behind the lacy bedroom curtains. He was well dressed, and carried an umbrella. An umbrella? Perhaps it was a cane.

Spence said, "I seem to be seeing, more and more, these people—people I don't think are truly there."

"*He's* there."

"I think they're dead. Dead people."

His wife drew back and cast him a sidelong glance, smiling mysteriously. "It does seem to have upset you," she said.

"Since I know they're not there—"

"*He's* there."

"—so I must be losing my mind. A kind of schizophrenia, waking dreams, hallucinations—"

Spence was speaking excitedly, and did not know exactly what he was saying. His wife drew away from him in alarm, or distaste.

119

"You take everything so personally," she said.

One morning shortly after the New Year, when the air was sharp as a knife, and the sky so blue it brought tears of pain to one's eyes, Spence set off on the underground route from his train station to his building. Beneath the city's paved surface was a honeycomb of tunnels, some of them damp and befouled but most of them in good condition, with, occasionally, a corridor of gleaming white tiles that looked as if it had been lovingly polished by hand. Spence preferred aboveground, or believed he should prefer aboveground, for reasons vague and puritanical, but in fierce weather he made his way underground, and worried only that he might get lost, as he sometimes did. (Yet, even lost, he had only to find an escalator or steps leading to the street—and he was no longer lost.)

This morning, however, the tunnels were far more crowded than usual. Spence saw a preponderance of elderly men and women, with here and there a young face, startling, and seemingly unnatural. Here and there, yet more startling, a child's face. Very few of the faces had that air, so disconcerting to him in the past, of the eerily familiar laid upon the utterly unfamiliar; and these he resolutely ignored.

He soon fell into step with the crowd, keeping to their pace—which was erratic, surging, faster along straight stretches of tunnel and slower at curves; he found it agreeable to be borne along by the flow, as of a tide. A tunnel of familiar tear-stained mosaics yielded to one of the smart gleaming tunnels and that in turn to a tunnel badly in need of repair—and, indeed, being noisily repaired, by one of those crews of workmen that labor at all hours of the day and night beneath the surface of the city—and as Spence hurried past the deafening vibrations of the air hammer he found himself descending stairs into a tunnel unknown to him: a place of warm, humming, droning sound, like conversation, though none of his fellow pedestrians seemed to be talking. Where were they going, so many people? And in the same direction?—with only, here and there, a lone, clearly lost individual bucking the tide, white-faced, eyes snatching at his as if in desperate recognition.

Might as well accompany them, Spence thought, and see.

The Language of Love

by Lisa DePaulo

It's hard to believe how difficult life is for some children. Joanie Hughes found that out. She decided she had to rescue one child, as we learn in this true account.

Deaf since birth, Sonya Kinney was long neglected by her parents. Then she met Joanie Hughes, a devoted interpreter who gave her a real home—and a chance to be heard.

It was seven years ago that Joanie Hughes first laid eyes on Sonya Kinney.

She was a tiny little thing, sitting at a table in the back of her second-grade classroom, coloring away—while all the other 7-year-olds gathered in the front, listening to the teacher read a story.

Hughes sat down beside her.

"Hi," she said, her fingers forming words in sign language. "I'm your interpreter, Joanie Hughes."

The girl looked up with big brown doe eyes, and grinned. "She looked like a little elf," remembers Hughes. Her two front teeth were missing and her hair was chopped short—sticking up in some spots, bare to the scalp in others—as if someone had taken scissors and just hacked away. From her ears, two hearing aids stuck out like marbles. Her clothes were stained and soiled, her sneakers ripped. When they went out for recess, her dirty coat barely fit.

"But she had this big smile and these big beautiful eyes." Eyes that spoke volumes, Hughes recalls. "She had this look of wide-eyed wonder, full of love and full of need."

Joanie Hughes was 42 at the time, a wife and mother of two girls just reaching adolescence. She taught sign language as part of a volunteer ministry at her church, and also worked full-time interpreting for students in public schools in Wilmington, N.C.—one of the few school systems in the country to integrate deaf and hearing students. Hughes had been assigned to the high school when she got a call that there was a problem at Bradley Creek Elementary. Two deaf second graders had been without an interpreter for a month; they needed her badly. Oh, and there was one other problem. The little girl had missed 12 days of school because of head lice.

Hughes's other charge was a boy named Daniel, adorable in a crisp white shirt and pressed jeans, clutching a lunch box. "Sonya had nothing," Hughes remembers, nothing but a huge smile and a nearly insatiable hunger for attention. So relieved was she to have someone to "talk" to that her tiny fingers moved nonstop, telling all kinds of stories to Hughes. "She had such an excitement for life," says Hughes, "when she really had no reason to."

At the end of the first day, Sonya's eyes filled with tears, and what she said with her fingers broke Hughes's heart:

"Can I come home with you, Miss Joanie?"

Seven years later, Sonya Kinney would come home with Miss Joanie for good. In a landmark case that has raised serious issues about the rights of deaf children, a judge in North Carolina granted full custody of Sonya to Hughes. Sonya's parents, the judge ruled, had neglected her, most notably by refusing to learn sign language.

The case was extraordinary for several reasons: It's highly unusual for a nonbiological "parent" to gain custody of a teenager, particularly when both parents are alive and the child has three siblings who have not been removed from the household. But more unusual—and important to deaf children—was that, for the first time, the failure of parents to communicate with their children was considered neglect.

But Judge Shelly Holt did not base her decision solely on the parents' failure to learn to sign. There were horrific conditions that would be difficult for any child to endure. But it was even more difficult for a child who could not express herself—except to Hughes, who for seven years would learn about the abuse suffered by this child who had crept into her life and heart.

"It's frightening to think of" what might have become of Sonya had she not met Joanie Hughes. "But I'm the lucky one," says Hughes. "Sonya is an extraordinary child."

Ironically, it was Joanie Hughes's love for her yet-unborn child that made her learn sign language. She was pregnant with her second daughter, Kelli, now 19, while she was teaching Sunday school. A couple of kids had German measles and, Hughes learned, her exposure to them could mean a loss of hearing for her baby. Taking no chances, Hughes began to learn to sign before Kelli was born—healthy, with no hearing impairment. "I thought the Lord was going to give me a deaf child," says Hughes, in her sweet, soft voice, her hazel eyes moist with tears. "And He did, but it wasn't Kelli."

Hughes took her new skill and helped deaf children while her girls were still babies. She even raised her daughters in a "bilingual" home, teaching them American Sign Language as they learned to speak. "I just thought it was a wonderful language for anyone to know."

As an interpreter, Hughes had always tried not to blur the lines of professionalism. But Sonya was needier than any student Hughes had ever met. Every day for the first week after they met, Sonya would ask, "Can I come to your house? My mama will let me. Please, Miss Joanie, please."

Hughes had her husband of 24 years, not to mention her own two daughters to think about. Kelli was then 11; Traci, 13. Hughes wasn't sure they could handle their mommy showering affection on another child. So she had a talk with them. How would they feel, she asked, if she brought this little girl home to meet them? They said it was fine—and when they met Sonya, they understood why their mother felt the way she did.

So began a relationship that would change all their lives.

Sonya's parents, Norman Kinney and Christyne ("Leann") Kinney Estes, had separated a year or so before, and Sonya was living with her mother in an old trailer with a rusty door and broken steps. When Hughes called Estes to ask if she could take Sonya out, she replied, "I don't care." What time should she bring her home? "I don't care." When Hughes went to pick her up the first time, she wondered for a moment if this was such a good idea. But then, through a dirty window in the trailer, she saw Sonya watching for her with those big hopeful eyes.

"Sonya ran up and started hugging me, saying, 'You're really taking me skating!'" Beside her, a cute little boy was sitting quietly on the couch. He was Sonya's twin, Jonathan. "Would you like to come too?" Hughes asked. "Yes, ma'am!" he said and ran to get his jacket.

Soon Sonya—her fingers aflutter—was sharing stories about her home. What astounded Hughes was that she'd relay frightening goings-on matter-of-factly: "Mama and Daddy had a fight and Mama kicked Daddy out and busted his nose, ha, ha." Or: "I'm not gonna tell Mama about the bugs anymore cause I'm scared I'm gonna burn up." Hughes asked what she meant. "Mama puts gas on my head and Daddy say he's gonna take his cigarette lighter and get rid of 'em once and for all."

Hughes later learned she was not the first to be alarmed by the conditions in Sonya's household. Others had reported the family to social services, who at one point, years earlier, had removed Sonya from Estes's care. But she was soon allowed to go back home.

Hughes took Sonya and Jonathan out a few times before she met Estes. It happened one day when the school called Estes in because Sonya had a particularly bad case of lice. "Her mother walks in in a Harley-Davidson T-shirt with a pack of cigarettes rolled up in one sleeve. And Sonya runs over and hugs her," Hughes remembers. Hughes extended her hand and said, "I'm so glad to finally meet you." Estes's reply: "I'm so mad about this school calling me all the time, making me come pick up this young 'un."

"And she just dragged her off. No good-bye, no thank you. I wanted to run out that door and grab her and say: 'You don't deserve this child.'"

But Hughes bit her lip; she was only the interpreter. And in fact she served in that official capacity only briefly; after a few months the district had hired another interpreter for the elementary school and sent Hughes back to her post at the high school. That could have been the end of their relationship. But by that point, Hughes cared too deeply for Sonya to even fathom not having the little girl in her life.

That first Christmas, the Hugheses bought Sonya a pile of clothes and toys. "When Sonya came back to school, I asked her why she wasn't wearing any of the new clothes," remembers Hughes. "Sonya answered, 'Oh, Mama had to sell them. She needed milk and food and beer.'"

Hughes was furious. But Estes was her mama—and Hughes had to remember that. Eventually, Hughes learned the hard way what Estes would do if she thought Hughes had overstepped her bounds. Once, when Sonya was 11, Estes refused to let Sonya visit Hughes for a few months. During that time, Sonya called Hughes constantly from a pay phone down the street, crying hysterically.

Estes and Hughes lived only a few miles apart in the tiny town of Wilmington. It's nestled between the shores of Wrightsville Beach and the Cape Fear River, a town so beautiful that it's not unusual to see Hollywood film crews there. But like many resort areas, it also has a section that's poor to middle-class at best.

Hughes's modest ranch home was within walking distance of most of the trailer parks. Estes moved her family—Sonya, Jonathan, and two older girls, KaNesha and Consuelo—six times over eight years, usually after not paying her bills. And every weekend, when Hughes would pick up Sonya, there seemed to be a new set of deplorable conditions.

But except for those months when she was cut off from Hughes, Sonya always had a refuge. She spent almost every weekend with Joanie Hughes, snuggled in a pretty pink bed filled with stuffed animals. At Hughes's house, Sonya could talk to her friends on the phone (with a TDD, a computer hookup that allows messages to be typed or relayed by an operator) and watch her favorite television shows (via a closed-captioned set). The Hugheses would take her skating and help with schoolwork. Then on Sunday, Hughes would bring Sonya back. The whole while, Hughes repeatedly offered to teach Estes sign language. "I told her I would teach both her and the father for free. But they wanted no part of it. There's a one-hand sign for 'I love you' and they wouldn't even learn that."

"I'm her mama," Estes would tell her, "and she's gotta learn to talk." This was not an unusual reaction at one time; hearing parents of deaf children were often told, incorrectly, by teachers and doctors, that their children would never talk if they relied on sign language.

Estes, who was on welfare, rarely had a phone, let alone a TDD. Despite Sonya's monthly Social Security check of $458, Estes never spent the money on anything to help her daughter communicate. Estes's only way of communicating with Sonya was by scribbling notes—usually when she had chores for her to do.

As her siblings got older, Sonya felt increasingly isolated. "They'd be out with their friends, and I'd be sitting home alone with nobody to talk to, and missing Miss Joanie." When she neared adolescence, it was Hughes who told Sonya that she'd soon be getting her period, believing that if she didn't explain, Sonya wouldn't know what was happening.

Remarkably, she did extremely well in school—almost always earning A's—due in no small part to the help she got from the Hughes family. But she is also an extraordinarily bright child, with an optimism that is almost palpable. "It's no big deal," Sonya signs. "I like school."

But in the spring of 1993, Sonya began having trouble in school and her normally cheery disposition crumbled. Hughes sensed something beyond the usual difficulties. The situation finally came to a head one weekend in April when Hughes picked up Sonya at the bus stop.

"Normally, the school bus would pull up and she'd be at the window, waving and smiling," says Hughes. "She was always the first kid off. This time, she was the last. I thought, Uh-oh, something's wrong."

Something was very wrong.

Her mother's new husband, Billy, was touching her, Sonya explained, the tears running down her cheeks. He would come into the bathroom when she was in the shower, but Sonya would scream. He would come into her room at night when she was asleep, but he'd leave when her screams woke Jonathan, who slept in the same room. Yet there were lots of times when Sonya was alone in the house and no amount of screaming would matter. "He assumed that, being deaf, who's she gonna tell?" says Hughes.

And he was partly right. The abuse went on for almost six months but Sonya literally couldn't tell her mother. "I tried," says Sonya, "but she didn't understand." She could, however, tell Joanie Hughes, who sat with her that day and wept.

126

By this point Hughes's marriage had ended in divorce and she was a single mother of two teenagers. She knew she had to do something decisive to help Sonya. So she reported the abuse to social services, who called Estes and told her to have Billy leave, or risk losing Sonya. Estes kicked him out and called Hughes to come over and interpret for her and Norman Kinney Sonya's version of events. "They got all mad," Hughes remembers, "and they were going to go find Billy and beat him up." But they never called the police. (No charges were ever brought against him; he died of cancer soon after.)

By this time, Kinney had started to get on his feet financially and decided he wanted his kids. He and Estes had an unusual custody agreement: The kids would spend alternate years with mother and father. Kinney never took them for his years, though, in large part because he was usually broke, as he later admitted in court. But when he got a job painting and renovating for an elderly couple, the Hansons, he moved into their basement. When the Hansons met his children, they were so touched that they offered to rent him their extra rooms upstairs. Finally, Hughes felt, the family had a chance.

That Christmas she, Traci, and Kelli decided that, instead of ex-changing gifts, they'd buy presents for Sonya, Jonathan, KaNesha, Consuelo, and even for Kinney. They put his name on some of the gifts, so the kids would think their father had bought them. Kinney, too, bought presents—but with the money he got from pawning some of the Hansons' belongings (he was later convicted of larceny). After Christmas, Kinney moved out with the kids to an apartment of his own.

Still, nearly every weekend Sonya came to visit.

Her stories had now changed—but were equally upsetting. "Daddy promised me if I lived with him he would stop drinking," says Sonya, "but then he broke his promise."

"She'd call me when she'd come home from school," says Hughes. "She'd be alone in the apartment, with no one to help her with her homework. And when Norman did arrive he would immediately start drinking." Kinney was now receiving Sonya's Social Security check, but it still wasn't being spent on her special needs.

When Sonya would protest, he'd call her "retard"—later explaining in court that he didn't see what the big deal was, since he "called all his kids 'retard.'" When she was little and he wanted her attention, he'd stomp his feet. And when he got a painting job, he'd promised Sonya money for helping, but it never came through. "She was like a mini slave," says Hughes.

Hughes tried to give Kinney the benefit of the doubt. But rarely did a few days pass without a call from a crying Sonya, sometimes from the Dairy Mart down the street. At those times, she'd ask a clerk to read a note, or talk herself in the severely muted way that Hughes alone could understand. In either case, the message was the same: "Pick me up! Everybody's gone and Daddy's drunk."

"So I'd pick her up, give her a meal, and, when he was sober, bring her back." But even when her father was sober, Sonya was still not properly cared for. At one point, for instance, her breast was sore, but she didn't feel she could communicate that to her father. She told Hughes, who immediately had her checked. A lump was found and Sonya had surgery to remove a benign cyst. Hughes called Estes, but she never showed up at the hospital or even phoned.

Finally, Sonya begged Hughes to let her move in. Hughes encouraged her to give her father another chance. Then one day after church—Hughes took her almost every Sunday—Sonya asked to see the preacher. With Hughes interpreting, she told him, "I want you to pray for me because if I have to keep living with my Daddy, I'm gonna die."

Hughes appealed to Kinney, who said, Hughes recalls, "Fine, take her. You always wanted her anyway."

And suddenly all was calm. But it was not to last.

A few weeks after an ecstatic Sonya moved in, Hughes says that Kinney called, saying, "She's gotta come home. The deal's off." Later, in court, Hughes's lawyer tried to show that the change of heart was the result of Kinney's realizing that if he didn't have Sonya, he wouldn't get her monthly Social Security check. Kinney denied this. But this time Hughes, at Sonya's urging, said, "Norman, I'm not bringing Sonya home."

A few weeks later Kinney sent the police, but Sonya begged the officers, with Traci and Kelli translating, to let her stay. "The police were very sensitive," says Hughes. They didn't take her away, but they did advise Hughes to immediately contact social services.

The local family services agency did an investigation and concluded that Sonya was not abused or neglected.

Undeterred, Hughes went to legal services and found a lawyer. When Jim Morgan first heard her story over the phone, he thought: A nonparent seeking custody, the county has already found no abuse or neglect, all the case law is against her.

But something made him agree to meet her. Hughes brought Sonya along.

"And this incredible little girl, with this lady interpreting, started telling me all that had happened," says Morgan. "It was so compelling and emotional that I was, like, oh, man. I've gotta do something." He took the case for free.

In an office across town, another lawyer, John Burns, felt equally compelled to represent Kinney, whom he felt was a victim of class warfire. "Norman is a North Carolina country boy. And that means he talks and lives in certain ways that put him at a disadvantage," says Burns. He believed that Kinney should retain primary custody.

The custody trial took three heart-wrenching days in May, 1995. Traci and Kelli Hughes sat in the front row, holding Sonya's hands. On the stand, Kinney came across as more pathetic than malicious. He admitted to his drinking and his "million" broken promises to Sonya. He said he had refused to learn to sign because he felt guilty and could never face up to her disability. There was a history of mental illness in his family, he explained. "I thought it might be generic [sic] or something."

Sonya's siblings were in a difficult spot—they testified on Kinney's behalf, alienating Sonya, who feels they down-played their father's drinking, in the hope of keeping Sonya home. But their presence also raised a troubling question: If Kinney's home was bad, why shouldn't they be removed too?

Judge Holt made it clear in her decision that while there was much amiss in the household, the situation had taken a particularly heavy toll on Sonya because of her deafness; her father's refusal to communicate with her constituted neglect.

But at least her father had fought for her. Leann Estes didn't even show up. When Judge Holt announced her decision, a sobbing Sonya signed to Hughes, "You saved my life." Then she ran up to the bench and reached for Judge Holt; the judge leaned over and held her hands.

Strangely silent in the wake of the decision were advocacy groups for the deaf, who had been reluctant to take a stand on the case. This is partly due to the warring factions—those who believe that deaf people should sign as a primary language versus those who believe they should learn to speak.

But the main reason the groups are mum is that a great many deaf kids have parents who do not sign. As Kathryn Meadow-Orlans, a senior research scientist at Gallaudet University (the only liberal arts university exclusively for deaf students), puts it, "To suggest that nonsigning parents are abusing their deaf children would be a travesty." More than 90 percent of all deaf children are born to hearing parents, and a great many of those parents do not learn or are not fluent in sign language. Still, studies show that deaf kids whose parents do learn to sign consistently and well, when the child is young, fare far better in terms of academic achievement and social adjustment.

"This case should be a wake-up call," says Gallaudet anthropologist Carol Erting, "especially to schools, which have to realize that it's critical to help families get the skills they need. And also to help them through the grieving process—that they do have a deaf child and they need to make accommodations. Some parents get that right away. Many never do."

On Mother's Day, Sonya picked out a card for her "old mama" as she calls Leann Estes and brought it to her doorstep. She got no reply. Sonya calls Hughes her "new mama" and has started calling herself Sonya Kinney-Hughes. She plans to have it legally changed. She has not seen her father since his larceny trial last July.

The real losers may be Sonya's siblings. Sonya has seen Jonathan just once since last May, when he showed up at the skating rink on a Saturday night. The reunion was sad and emotional. "He cried when we were leaving," says Hughes, who wanted to bring him to dinner. "I can't," he told Sonya. "Daddy's still mad at Miss Joanie."

As Sonya's legal guardian, Hughes was finally able to get the girl's medical records. She knew Sonya had been deaf since birth, and could hear only slight vibrations in one ear. But she'd hoped all along that something could be done to enhance her "good ear." Although a specialist said nothing could be done surgically, Sonya was fitted with vastly improved hearing aids that enable her to detect some sounds (a cricket recently took her by surprise) and will ultimately help her pronounce more clearly when she does speak.

But when Hughes first read the medical records, she sobbed. At birth Sonya weighed only two pounds, two ounces. At 7 months, she had an operation to help her breathe. A doctor had written on her chart that her lips were blue and she was malnourished. He later noted: "Mother visits child one time in 20 days."

"From the very beginning . . ." Hughes says, crying.

It's Saturday night in Wrightsville Beach and Sonya, who can pick up the beat of the music, is doing a perfect spin around the Showtime Skating Rink.

"Hey, Mama," Sonya signs to Hughes as she skates, "my favorite song!"

Hughes beams.

"Mama, look!" says Sonya, as she does a pirouette. Beside her, smiling broadly and signing with her is Daniel, Hughes's other pupil from seven years ago. "My two little second graders," says Hughes, proudly. "Now they're in driver's ed together!"

"Okay, ladies' choice!" says the announcer, cuing up the next song.

Hughes signs the message to Sonya, who flashes a huge smile that expresses all the emotions her hands can't. Not that she needs any words as she skates off the rink and runs to grab her mama's hand.

Hughes is Sonya's choice.

131

What's Alien You?

by Dave Barry

If the Earth were visited by aliens, that would be serious business—right? Sometimes it seems that Dave Barry can't take anything seriously. Or is he correct this time? Will we take the right action when faced with destruction by aliens who enjoy soap operas?

I don't want to alarm anybody, but there is an excellent chance that the Earth will be destroyed in the next several days. Congress is thinking about eliminating a federal program under which scientists broadcast signals to alien beings. This would be a large mistake. Alien beings have atomic blaster death cannons. You cannot cut off their federal programs as if they were merely poor people.

I realize that some of you may not believe that alien beings exist. But how else can you explain the many unexplained phenomena that people are always sighting, such as lightning and flying saucers? Oh, I know the authorities claim these sightings are actually caused by "weather balloons," but that is a bucket of manure if I ever heard one. (That's just a figure of speech, of course. I realize that manure is silent.)

Answer this question honestly: Have you, or has any member of your immediate family, ever seen a weather balloon? Of course not.

132

Nobody has. Yet if these so-called authorities were telling the truth, the skies over America would be dark with weather balloons. Commercial aviation would be impossible. Nevertheless, the authorities trot out this tired old explanation, or an even stupider one, every time a flying saucer is sighted:

> *New York—Authorities say that the gigantic, luminous object flying at tremendous speeds in the skies of Manhattan last night, which was reported by more than seven million people, including the mayor, a Supreme Court justice, several bishops, and thousands of airline pilots, brain surgeons, and certified public accountants, was simply an unusual air-mass inversion. "That's all it was, an air-mass inversion," said the authorities, in unison. Asked why the people also reported seeing the words "WE ARE ALIEN BEINGS WHO COME IN PEACE WITH CURES FOR ALL YOUR MAJOR DISEASES AND A CARBURETOR THAT GETS 450 MILES PER GALLON HIGHWAY ESTIMATE" written on the side of the object in letters over three hundred feet tall, the authorities replied, "Well, it could also have been a weather balloon."*

Wake up, America! There are no weather balloons! Those are alien beings! They are all around us! I'm sure most of you have seen the movie *E.T.*, which is the story of an alien who almost dies when he falls into the clutches of the American medical-care establishment, but is saved by preadolescent boys. Everybody believes that the alien is a fake, a triumph of special effects. But watch the movie closely next time. The alien is real! The *boys* are fakes! *Real* preadolescent boys would have beaten the alien to death with rocks.

Yes, aliens do exist. And high government officials know they exist but have been keeping this knowledge top secret. Here is the Untold Story:

Years ago, when the alien-broadcast program began, government scientists decided to broadcast a message that would be simple, yet would convey a sense of love, universal peace, and brotherhood: "Have a nice day." They broadcast this message over and over, day after day, year after year, until one day they got an answer:

DEAR EARTH PERSONS:
OKAY. WE ARE HAVING A NICE DAY. WE ALSO HAVE A
NUMBER OF EXTREMELY SOPHISTICATED WEAPONS, AND
UNLESS YOU START BROADCASTING SOMETHING MORE
INTERESTING, WE WILL REDUCE YOUR PLANET TO A VERY
WARM OBJECT THE SIZE OF A CHILD'S BOWLING BALL.
REGARDS,
THE ALIENS

So the scientists, desperate for something that would interest the
aliens, broadcast an episode of "I Love Lucy," and the aliens *loved* it.
They demanded more, and soon they were getting all three major net-
works, and the Earth was saved. There is only one problem: *the aliens
have terrible taste.* They love game shows, soap operas, Howard
Cosell, and "Dallas." Whenever a network tries to take one of these
shows off the air, the aliens threaten to vaporize the planet.

This is why you and all your friends think television is awful. It isn't
designed to please you: it's designed to please creatures from another
galaxy. You know the Wisk commercial, the one with the ring around
the collar, the one that is so spectacularly stupid that it makes you
wonder why anybody would dream of buying the product? Well, the
aliens *love* that commercial. We all owe a great debt of gratitude to
the people who make Wisk. They have not sold a single bottle of Wisk
in fourteen years, but they have saved the earth.

Very few people know any of this. Needless to say, the congress has
no idea what is going on. Most congressmen are incapable of eating
breakfast without the help of several aides, so we can hardly expect
them to understand a serious threat from outer space. But if they go
ahead with their plan to cancel the alien-broadcast program, and the
aliens miss the next episode of "General Hospital," what do you think
will happen? Think about it and have a nice day.

Future Tense

by Robert Lipsyte

Gary thought he was being clever. He didn't realize just how clever he was ...

G ary couldn't wait for tenth grade to start so he could strut his sentences, parade his paragraphs, renew his reputation as the top creative writer in school. At the opening assembly, he felt on edge, psyched, like a boxer before the first-round bell. He leaned forward as Dr. Proctor, the principal, introduced two new staff members. He wasn't particularly interested in the new vice-principal, Ms. Jones; Gary never had discipline problems, he'd never even had to stay after school. But his head cocked alertly as Dr. Proctor introduced the new Honors English teacher, Mr. Smith. Here was the person he'd have to impress.

He studied Mr. Smith. The man was hard to describe. He looked as though he'd been manufactured to fit his name. Average height, brownish hair, pale white skin, medium build. Middle age. He was the sort of person you began to forget the minute you met him. Even his clothes had no particular style. They merely covered his body.

Mr. Smith was . . . just there.

Gary was studying Mr. Smith so intently that he didn't hear Dr. Proctor call him up to the stage to receive an award from last term. Jim Baggs jabbed an elbow into his ribs and said, "Let's get up there, Dude."

Dr. Proctor shook Gary's hand and gave him the County Medal for Best Composition. While Dr. Proctor was giving Jim Baggs the County Trophy for Best All-Round Athlete, Gary glanced over his shoulder to see if Mr. Smith looked impressed. But he couldn't find the new teacher. Gary wondered if Mr. Smith was so ordinary he was invisible when no one was talking about him.

On the way home, Dani Belzer, the prettiest poet in school, asked Gary, "What did you think of our new Mr. Wordsmith?"

"If he was a color he'd be beige," said Gary. "If he was a taste he'd be water. If he was a sound he'd be a low hum."

"Fancy, empty words," sneered Mike Chung, ace reporter on the school paper. "All you've told me is you've got nothing to tell me."

Dani quickly stepped between them. "What did you think of the first assignment?"

"Describe a Typical Day at School," said Gary, trying unsuccessfully to mimic Mr. Smith's bland voice. "That's about as exciting as tofu."

"A real artist," said Dani, "accepts the commonplace as a challenge."

That night, hunched over his humming electric typewriter, Gary wrote a description of a typical day at school from the viewpoint of a new teacher who was seeing everything for the very first time, who took nothing for granted. He described the shredded edges of the limp flag outside the dented front door, the worn flooring where generations of kids had nervously paced outside the principal's office, the nauseatingly sweet pipe-smoke seeping out of the teachers' lounge.

And then, in the last line, he gave the composition that extra twist, the little kicker on which his reputation rested. He wrote:

> The new teacher's beady little eyes missed nothing, for they were the optical recorders of an alien creature who had come to earth to gather information.

The next morning, when Mr. Smith asked for a volunteer to read aloud, Gary was on his feet and moving toward the front of the classroom before Mike Chung got his hand out of his pocket.

136

The class loved Gary's composition. They laughed and stamped their feet. Chung shrugged, which meant he couldn't think of any criticism, and Dani flashed thumbs up. Best of all, Jim Baggs shouldered Gary against the blackboard after class and said, "Awesome tale, Dude."

Gary felt good until he got the composition back. Along one margin, in a perfect script, Mr. Smith had written:

You can do better.

"How would he know?" Gary complained on the way home.

"You should be grateful," said Dani. "He's pushing you to the farthest limits of your talent."

"Which may be nearer than you think," snickered Mike.

Gary rewrote his composition, expanded it, complicated it, thickened it. Not only was this new teacher an alien, he was part of an extraterrestrial conspiracy to take over Earth. Gary's final sentence was:

> Every iota of information, fragment of fact, morsel of minutiae sucked up by those vacuuming eyes was beamed directly into a computer circling the planet. The data would eventually become a program that would control the mind of every school kid on earth.

Gary showed the new draft to Dani before class. He stood on tiptoes so he could read over her shoulder. Sometimes he wished she were shorter, but mostly he wished he were taller.

"What do you think?"

"The assignment was to describe a typical day," said Dani. "This is off the wall."

He snatched the papers back. "Creative writing means creating." He walked away, hurt and angry. He thought: *If she doesn't like my compositions, how can I ever get her to like me?*

That morning, Mike Chung read his own composition aloud to the class. He described a typical day through the eyes of a student in a wheelchair. Everything most students take for granted was an obstacle: the bathroom door too heavy to open, the gym steps too steep to climb, the light switch too high on the wall. The class applauded and Mr. Smith nodded approvingly. Even Gary had to admit it was really good—if you considered plain-fact journalism as creative writing, that is.

Gary's rewrite came back the next day marked:

Improving. Try again.

Saturday he locked himself in his room after breakfast and rewrote the rewrite. He carefully selected his nouns and verbs and adjectives. He polished and arranged them in sentences as a jeweler strings pearls. He felt good as he wrote, as the electric typewriter hummed and buzzed and sometimes coughed. He thought: *Every champion knows that as hard as it is to get to the top, it's even harder to stay up there.*

His mother knocked on his door around noon. When he let her in, she said, "It's a beautiful day."

"Big project," he mumbled. He wanted to avoid a distracting conversation.

She smiled. "If you spend too much time in your room, you'll turn into a mushroom."

He wasn't listening. "Thanks. Anything's okay. Don't forget the mayonnaise."

Gary wrote:

> The alien's probes trembled as he read the student's composition. Could that skinny, bespectacled earthling really suspect its extraterrestrial identity? Or was his composition merely the result of a creative thunderstorm in a brilliant young mind?

Before Gary turned in his composition on Monday morning, he showed it to Mike Chung. He should have known better.

"You're trying too hard," chortled Chung. "Truth is stronger than fiction."

Gary flinched at that. It hurt. It might be true. But he couldn't let his competition know he had scored. "You journalists are stuck in the present and the past," growled Gary. "Imagination prepares us for what's going to happen."

Dani read her composition aloud to the class. It described a typical day from the perspective of a louse choosing a head of hair to nest in. The louse moved from the thicket of a varsity crew-cut to the matted jungle of a sagging perm to a straight, sleek blond cascade.

The class cheered and Mr. Smith smiled. Gary felt a twinge of jealousy. Dani and Mike were coming on. There wasn't room for more than one at the top.

In the hallway, he said to Dani, "And you called my composition off the wall?"

Mike jumped in. "There's a big difference between poetical metaphor and hack science fiction."

Gary felt choked by a lump in his throat. He hurried away.

Mr. Smith handed back Gary's composition the next day marked:
See me after school.

Gary was nervous all day. What was there to talk about? Maybe Mr. Smith hated science fiction. One of those traditional English teachers. Didn't understand that science fiction could be literature. *Maybe I can educate him,* thought Gary.

When Gary arrived at the English office, Mr. Smith seemed nervous too. He kept folding and unfolding Gary's composition. "Where do you get such ideas?" he asked in his monotone voice.

Gary shrugged. "They just come to me."

"Alien teachers. Taking over the minds of schoolchildren." Mr. Smith's empty eyes were blinking. "What made you think of that?"

"I've always had this vivid imagination."

"If you're sure it's just your imagination." Mr. Smith looked relieved. "I guess everything will work out." He handed back Gary's composition. "No more fantasy, Gary. Reality. That's your assignment. Write only about what you know."

Outside school, Gary ran into Jim Baggs, who looked surprised to see him. "Don't tell me you had to stay after, Dude."

"I had to see Mr. Smith about my composition. He didn't like it. Told me to stick to reality."

"Don't listen." Jim Baggs body-checked Gary into the schoolyard fence. "Dude, you got to be yourself."

Gary ran all the way home and locked himself into his room. He felt feverish with creativity. Dude, you got to be yourself, Dude. It doesn't matter what your so-called friends say, or your English teacher. You've got to play your own kind of game, write your own kind of stories.

The words flowed out of Gary's mind and through his fingers and out of the machine and onto sheets of paper. He wrote and rewrote until he felt the words were exactly right:

With great effort, the alien shut down the electrical panic impulses coursing through its system and turned

139

on Logical Overdrive. There were two possibilities:

1. This high school boy was exactly what he seemed to be, a brilliant, imaginative, apprentice best-selling author and screenwriter, or,

2. He had somehow stumbled onto the secret plan and he would have to be either enlisted into the conspiracy or erased off the face of the planet.

First thing in the morning, Gary turned in his new rewrite to Mr. Smith. A half hour later, Mr. Smith called Gary out of Spanish. There was no expression on his regular features. He said, "I'm going to need some help with you."

Cold sweat covered Gary's body as Mr. Smith grabbed his arm and led him to the new vice-principal. She read the composition while they waited. Gary got a good look at her for the first time. Ms. Jones was . . . just there. She looked as though she'd been manufactured to fit her name. Average. Standard. Typical. The cold sweat turned into goose pimples.

How could he have missed the clues? Smith and Jones were aliens! He had stumbled on their secret and now they'd have to deal with him.

He blurted, "Are you going to enlist me or erase me?"

Ms. Jones ignored him. "In my opinion, Mr. Smith, you are over-reacting. This sort of nonsense"—she waved Gary's composition—"is the typical response of an overstimulated adolescent to the mixture of reality and fantasy in an environment dominated by manipulative music, television, and films. Nothing for us to worry about."

"If you're sure, Ms. Jones," said Mr. Smith. He didn't sound sure.

The vice-principal looked at Gary for the first time. There was no expression in her eyes. Her voice was flat. "You'd better get off this science fiction kick," she said. "If you know what's good for you."

"I'll never tell another human being, I swear," he babbled.

"What are you talking about?" asked Ms. Jones.

"Your secret is safe with me," he lied. He thought, *If I can just get away from them. Alert the authorities. Save the planet.*

"You see," said Ms. Jones, "you're writing yourself into a crazed state."

"You're beginning to believe your own fantasies," said Mr. Smith.

"I'm not going to do anything this time," said Ms. Jones, "but you must promise to write only about what you know."

"Or I'll have to fail you," said Mr. Smith.

"For your own good," said Ms. Jones. "Writing can be very dangerous."

"Especially for writers," said Mr. Smith, "who write about things they shouldn't."

"Absolutely," said Gary, "positively, no question about it. Only what I know." He backed out the door, nodding his head, thinking, *Just a few more steps and I'm okay. I hope these aliens can't read minds.*

Jim Baggs was practicing head fakes in the hallway. He slammed Gary into the wall with a hip block. "How's it going, Dude?" he asked, helping Gary up.

"Aliens," gasped Gary. "Told me no more science fiction."

"They can't treat a star writer like that," said Jim. "See what the head honcho's got to say." He grabbed Gary's wrist and dragged him to the principal's office.

"What can I do for you, boys?" boomed Dr. Proctor.

"They're messing with his moves, Doc," said Jim Baggs. "You got to let the aces run their paces."

"Thank you, James." Dr. Proctor popped his forefinger at the door. "I'll handle this."

"You're home free, Dude," said Jim, whacking Gary across the shoulder blades as he left.

"From the beginning," ordered Dr. Proctor. He nodded sympathetically as Gary told the entire story, from the opening assembly to the meeting with Mr. Smith and Ms. Jones. When Gary was finished, Dr. Proctor took the papers from Gary's hand. He shook his head as he read Gary's latest rewrite.

"You really have a way with words, Gary. I should have sensed you were on to something."

Gary's stomach flipped. "You really think there could be aliens trying to take over Earth?"

"Certainly," said Dr. Proctor, matter-of-factly. "Earth is the ripest plum in the universe."

Gary wasn't sure if he should feel relieved that he wasn't crazy or be scared out of his mind. He took a deep breath to control the quaver in his voice, and said: "I spotted Smith and Jones right away.

They look like they were manufactured to fit their names. Obviously humanoids. Panicked as soon as they knew I was on to them."

Dr. Proctor chuckled and shook his head. "No self-respecting civilization would send those two stiffs to Earth."

"They're not aliens?" He felt relieved and disappointed at the same time.

"I checked them out myself," said Dr. Proctor. "Just two average, standard, typical human beings, with no imagination, no creativity."

"So why'd you hire them?"

Dr. Proctor laughed. "Because they'd never spot an alien. No creative imagination. That's why I got rid of the last vice-principal and the last Honors English teacher. They were giving me odd little glances when they thought I wasn't looking. After ten years on your planet, I've learned to smell trouble."

Gary's spine turned to ice and dripped down the backs of his legs. "You're an alien!"

"Great composition," said Dr. Proctor, waving Gary's papers. "Grammatical, vividly written, and totally accurate."

"It's just a composition," babbled Gary, "made the whole thing up, imagination, you know."

Dr. Proctor removed the face of his wristwatch and began tapping tiny buttons. "Always liked writers. I majored in your planet's literature. Writers are the keepers of the past and the hope of the future. Too bad they cause so much trouble in the present."

"I won't tell anyone," cried Gary. "Your secret's safe with me." He began to back slowly toward the door.

Dr. Proctor shook his head. "How can writers keep secrets, Gary? It's their natures to share their creations with the world." He tapped three times and froze Gary in place, one foot raised to step out the door.

"But it was only a composition," screamed Gary as his body disappeared before his eyes.

"And I can't wait to hear what the folks back home say when you read it to them," said Dr. Proctor.

"I made it all up." Gary had the sensation of rocketing upward. "I made the whole . . ."

Icicle

by David Huddle

I smacked you in the mouth for no good reason
except that the icicle had broken off
so easily and that it felt like a club
in my hand, and so I swung it, the soft
pad of your lower lip sprouting a drop,
then gushing a trail onto the snow even
though we both squeezed the place with our fingers.
I'd give a lot not to be the swinger
of that icicle. I'd like another
morning just like that, cold, windy, and bright
as Russia, your glasses fogging up, your face
turning to me again. I tell you I might
help both our lives by changing that act to this,
by handing you the ice, a gift, my brother.

The Bermuda Triangle Mystery

by John Murray

Many people believe the Bermuda Triangle is a place with mysterious effects on ships and airplanes. Have people succumbed to fantasy—or is it really that way?

CHARACTERS

CAPTAIN MAYBERRY, *captain of* Enchantress
GLOVER, *first mate*
TURNER, *radio operator*
BILL ARMSTRONG, *owner of* Enchantress
MEG, *his wife*
LISA, *his teenage daughter*
MRS. ANNA BELLAMY, *his aunt*
AUDREY KENT, *a young widow*
PROFESSOR JANE SAMSON, *expert on psychic phenomena*
DAN PARSONS, *newspaperman*

TIME: *An evening in January.*
SETTING: *The foredeck and wheel room of the* Enchantress, *an*

144

ocean-going yacht. The deck is a triangular area downstage.
A rail borders the foredeck. The wheel room is at center on a
raised platform. It is reached from deck by a short ladder.
Wheel room has large spoked wheel, compass on a waist-
high stand, and table with radio equipment.
AT RISE: CAPTAIN MAYBERRY *stands at wheel.* TURNER, *wearing*
headphones, sits at radio. GLOVER *enters deck area from up*
right and climbs ladder to wheel room.

MAYBERRY: How's our course, Glover?

GLOVER: We're directly on course for Miami, Captain. We should arrive in about an hour, at twenty-two hundred.

MAYBERRY [*looking out over audience, as if studying ocean*]: If we make it through the Bermuda Triangle, you mean.

TURNER [*pushing back earphones*]: Are you superstitious, Captain?

MAYBERRY: I'm cautious. These waters can be treacherous. The sea is so calm . . . it's unusual for January. I don't like it.

GLOVER [*shaking his head*]: All the passengers are asking questions about the Bermuda Triangle. [*After a pause*] Captain, do you ever wonder about what's really out there?

MAYBERRY: I don't speculate, Glover. I'm a practical man. Whatever the stories, ships have sailed these waters for centuries and for millions of miles without incident. I only accept things I see and understand. [MRS. BELLAMY *enters up right, carrying knitting bag, and calls to wheel room.*]

MRS. BELLAMY [*waving bag*]: Oh, Admiral!

MAYBERRY [*exchanging amused looks with* GLOVER *and* TURNER]: It's Captain, ma'am.

MRS. BELLAMY: Whatever it is, when do we get to Miami?

MAYBERRY: In about an hour, Mrs. Bellamy.

MRS. BELLAMY: Thank goodness! I haven't had a moment's rest since I climbed onto this dreadful yacht. My nephew should find more important things to do than sail around this—this Devil's Triangle.

MAYBERRY: The Devil's Triangle is off the coast of Japan. We're off the coast of Florida, in the area called the Bermuda Triangle.

MRS. BELLAMY: All I know about this Triangle business is what I've read. [AUDREY KENT *enters left, unnoticed.*] People have disappeared here—without a trace.

145

MAYBERRY: You're right. The records go back a long time. Aaron Burr's daughter and her sailing party vanished over two hundred years ago.

MRS. BELLAMY [*confidentially*]: And what about poor Audrey Kent? Her husband vanished on that freighter five years ago, as though the sea had swallowed him. [AUDREY *steps forward.*]

AUDREY: Yes, Mrs. Bellamy, it was as though the sea swallowed him.

MRS. BELLAMY: Oh, Audrey... I didn't see you. [*Flustered*] I—I never would have mentioned it ...

AUDREY: It's quite all right, Mrs. Bellamy. I can talk freely about it now. [*Looking out over audience*] I don't know what happened to Jim and his ship—no one does—but someday I'll find the answer. That's why I came on this cruise. [*Pointing off right*] Look, that glow on the horizon must be Miami. [AUDREY *walks to railing, right.* GLOVER *joins her.* BILL ARMSTRONG, MEG, *and* LISA *enter up left.*]

LISA: Hi, Aunt Anna!

MRS. BELLAMY: Hello, Lisa, dear. Bill, I won't breathe easily until we get to Miami.

BILL: Relax, Aunt Anna. Enjoy the cruise. And the calm seas!

MRS. BELLAMY: Cruise indeed! I know what I know, and if you ask me, we shouldn't be here. There's something threatening about the Bermuda Triangle. [BILL *laughs.*]

MEG: Now, Aunt Anna, calm down. [*She and* BILL *sit.*]

LISA: I think it's romantic. [*She points.*] Look at that moon—and those stars.

MRS. BELLAMY [*grudgingly*]: If I were sixteen, I'd find it romantic, too. [*Sits.*]

LISA: It's so peaceful and calm. Everything is so still ... It's like waiting for the curtain to open on a play. Waiting for something to happen.

GLOVER [*joining them*]: The calm before the storm?

LISA [*nodding*]: Right. There's something all around us, and although I can't see it, I can feel its presence.

MRS. BELLAMY [*sharply*]: Stop talking like that, Lisa! You've been watching too many supernatural movies. You'll frighten me to death.

BILL [*heartily; putting arm around* MRS. BELLAMY]: Now, Aunt Anna, would I put my wife, my daughter, and my beloved aunt in danger? The *Enchantress* is unsinkable. [GLOVER *ascends ladder, relieves* MAYBERRY *at wheel.* MAYBERRY *stretches, descends ladder, joins group on deck.*]

MRS. BELLAMY: Well, of course you wouldn't ... but you're such a good PR man, I suppose you'd tell me all those missing ships were unsinkable, too.

BILL [*laughing*]: Good old Aunt Anna! You never miss a trick.

MRS. BELLAMY: Of course not. You've kept me on my toes ever since you were a little boy. [*Looks out.*] This sea is so vast. [*To* MAYBERRY] I simply cannot understand how you keep on course, Captain. Yet you claim we're headed directly for Miami.

MAYBERRY: There are many ways of finding our position. We can get an accurate reading from the stars. [*He points to wheel room.*] We have radio and radar. And I showed you the magnetic compass the other day.

MRS. BELLAMY: That thing with all the numerals and symbols?

MAYBERRY [*nodding*]: The compass needle points almost at a reading of the magnetic North Pole.

LISA: Almost? I thought the compass always points *at* the North Pole.

MAYBERRY: Not really. Compasses are never at a direct reading of true north. When a pilot charts a flight, he has to make allowances of almost 20 degrees for an off-course reading.

MRS. BELLAMY: Imagine that.

MAYBERRY: There are only two places in the world where the compass points directly north. The Devil's Triangle off Japan—and here, the Bermuda Triangle.

MEG: Why is that?

MAYBERRY [*smiling as he ascends ladder*]: No one has ever been able to explain it. If we knew the answer, we might be able to solve the mystery of the Bermuda Triangle. [DAN PARSONS *and* PROFESSOR JANE SAMSON *enter up left.*]

DAN [*to* JANE, *as they enter*]: Sorry, Jane, I just can't accept your theory. [*As dialogue continues,* MAYBERRY *relieves* GLOVER *at wheel.* GLOVER *rejoins* AUDREY *at railing, talking in pantomime.* TURNER *adjusts radio, studies charts on table up center.*] You can't really believe that there are hidden pockets in the atmosphere over the ocean where ships actually disappear. [*They walk toward group on deck.*]

JANE: It's possible, Dan. In a few short years we've learned more about space than we know about the sea. [DAN *shakes his head.*]

DAN: Time pockets—a twilight zone. It's too much for me. [*To others*] Hello, everyone.

BILL: Hello, Dan, Jane. It sounds as if you're in the midst of a heated scientific argument.

147

JANE [*laughing*]: Just a friendly discussion.

DAN [*to others*]: My paper has wanted an interview with the eminent Professor Samson for years. Her Bermuda Triangle theory is news.

LISA [*to Jane*]: Jane, I'll never forget what you told us about people who disappeared beyond a time barrier. Is it really possible?

JANE: I think it is, Lisa. I really believe there are numerous funnels or tunnels that are invisible, but can act as imprisoning sleeves. They can suck up people and vessels and whirl them on a course from north to south, depositing them in the vicinity of Antarctica—or beyond.

MRS. BELLAMY: I've never heard such nonsense.

BILL [*nodding*]: It *is* pretty farfetched.

LISA: I don't know, Dad. Something happened to all those people lost in the Bermuda Triangle. What about the five Army planes that went down without a trace, in 1945? And then the plane that went out searching for the missing planes was never heard from again, either.

MEG [*gesturing*]: Maybe a storm came up suddenly and destroyed them.

LISA: But, Mom, the planes were fully equipped with life rafts and jackets. Nothing was found—not even an oil slick, even though the Navy searched these waters for a month.

MRS. BELLAMY: Did that happen in this part of the ocean?

LISA [*nodding*]: Right off shore from Miami. [MRS. BELLAMY *shudders.*]

JANE [*smiling*]: I see you've been doing some research, Lisa. Those disappearances you mention just strengthen my theory. After all, Einstein taught us that time travels in a straight line. We all know that the Earth is shaped more like a pear than a globe, with indentations and grooves. Has time really compensated for the shape of the Earth? Can time actually pass over these spaces without having its effect?

MEG: These stories give me the willies.

JANE: Listen to this one: In 1941, a young pilot pulled out of a cloud bank, and found himself on a collision course with another plane. [MRS. BELLAMY *gasps in horror.*] The young pilot banked, but not before the other plane scraped his own craft. And the other plane was like a nightmare! The pilot later described it as World War One vintage, constructed of wood and canvas. Its pilot was wearing a leather flying helmet and goggles.

LISA [*giggling nervously*]: It sounds like the Red Baron.

JANE: When the young pilot landed, he reported the incident to the

Civil Aeronautics Board, but no such plane was on record anywhere as flying in the area. [*Others ad lib surprise.*] A few months after that, an ancient plane just like the one the young pilot described was found not far away in a barn.

DAN: That explains it! Somebody was having a good time in an unlicensed plane.

JANE: There's more. The CAB established that the old plane had been in the same position, untouched, for many years.

MRS. BELLAMY: Good heavens!

JANE: And they found a log book in the old plane. In the last entry its pilot noted coming upon a strange-looking silver aircraft that almost collided with him. Well, they put the log through a serious of tests, and authenticated its age. The entry was nearly fifty years old!

MEG: That's incredible!

JANE: Not only that. On the ancient plane, investigators found a long scrape along the side. Traces of the substance were tested and found to match up perfectly with the material used in the modern plane!

MEG: This is all just too weird. There has to be an explanation.

JANE [*slowly*]: I think the two planes met beyond the time barrier, two planes flying fifty years apart in time, but not in space.

DAN [*smirking*]: And where did all this take place—in Tibet?

JANE: No, Dan. Ohio!

MRS. BELLAMY [*standing*]: Well, I've had quite enough of your ghost stories! I'm retiring to my cabin until we reach Miami and a luxury hotel! [*She exits.*]

TURNER [*standing suddenly, waving a sheet of paper*]: Captain! Captain! What do you make of this?

MAYBERRY [*taking paper and reading aloud*]: "May Day, May Day. Caught in a whirlpool, sinking fast. Intense fog. Location 80 degrees west longitude . . ." [*Looking up*] Is that all, Turner?

TURNER: I lost contact, Captain. I'll try the distress frequency.

MAYBERRY: She didn't give her latitude reading. See if you can locate her on radar. [TURNER *nods.*] And call the Coast Guard at Miami. [TURNER *adjusts earphones and radio, pantomimes sending a message.*] Glover, take the wheel. [GLOVER *steps to wheel.*]

BILL: What's going on, Captain? Is it serious?

MAYBERRY [*moving to center*]: Afraid so. We've received word of a vessel in distress.

MEG: Oh, dear.

JANE: Did the ship give any identification?

MAYBERRY [*looking at paper*]: It's a vessel called the *Marie North*.

[AUDREY, *in great agitation, rushes up the ladder, shouting.*]

AUDREY: No! It can't be the *Marie North!* That was my husband's ship. It disappeared five years ago. [*Others move center.*]

BILL: Audrey, it must just be a coincidence. A ship with the same name.

AUDREY [*frantic*]: There couldn't be another ship named the *Marie North*. [*Hysterically*] It's Jim's ship, I tell you!

TURNER [*at radio*]: The Coast Guard orders us to stand by for further instructions. So far, there's no sign of the ship on radar. [TURNER *operates radio during following dialogue.*]

MAYBERRY [*grimly*]: We don't have enough fuel for an extensive search.

GLOVER: But the *Marie North* must be nearby. We received a clear, direct signal.

AUDREY: Yes, I know Jim is near. I've felt his presence all day.

BILL [*gesturing*]: Meg, Lisa, you'd better go to Aunt Anna's cabin and keep her company. I don't know how long we'll be delayed. [MEG *and* LISA *exit.*]

DAN: I guess I have quite a story here.

BILL: You'd better wait until we're certain of the facts.

JANE: Will we ever be certain?

MAYBERRY: One thing puzzles me. The *Marie North* mentioned "intense fog." [*He gestures.*] Yet we can see Miami. There's no fog within miles.

GLOVER [*frightened*]: Captain Mayberry! [*Everyone turns.*] Look at the compass! [*As* MAYBERRY *crosses to compass*] I've never seen anything like that.

MAYBERRY: The needle is spinning clockwise. It's gone crazy! [*Everyone looks at compass.*]

DAN [*whistling softly*]: It's going wild.

MAYBERRY: It's impossible to get a reading. [*Suddenly,* GLOVER'S *hands tremble. He struggles to maintain control of the wheel.*]

GLOVER: Captain!

MAYBERRY: What's wrong, Glover?

GLOVER [*straining*]: There's something pulling us. I—I can't control the wheel. [MAYBERRY *quickly joins him. They struggle to control wheel.*]

150

MAYBERRY [*straining*]: It—it feels as though we're being pulled backward!

[BILL *studies compass.*]

BILL: The needle is moving faster than ever.

JANE [*nodding*]: There's no reading at all.

AUDREY [*distracted*]: It's Jim. He's trying to find me. He wants me to join him on the *Marie North.*

DAN [*roughly*]: Stop it, Audrey! Pull yourself together. We're sailing through ocean turbulence, that's all.

[MAYBERRY *and* GLOVER *continue to strain at wheel.*]

MAYBERRY [*tense*]: I can hold it now, Glover. [GLOVER *relaxes, wipes brow.* MAYBERRY *takes wheel alone.*] Whatever it was, it's over.

GLOVER: We must have passed through some kind of strong cross-current.

TURNER [*calling*]: Captain, I still can't make contact with the *Marie North.*

MAYBERRY: Keep trying. Radio that help is on the way. Ask for a new fix on their position.

[TURNER *nods, returns to radio.* GLOVER *sways, grabs compass for support.*]

GLOVER: Help! [*Hoarsely*] Something's pulling at me. [*Hands remain on compass.*] I can barely stand up. [BILL *and* DAN *grab* GLOVER.]

DAN [*struggling*]: I feel it, too.

BILL: It's as though something is pulling my arms in opposite directions. Captain, can you manage the wheel?

MAYBERRY [*nodding*]: It's under control.

DAN: Then it must be a force from the compass. Try to let go, Glover. Let go! [*Straining,* GLOVER *finally pulls hands from compass. He sags against the table, breathing heavily.*]

GLOVER: I know it sounds crazy, but I was being pulled into the compass. It seemed as if it were alive!

BILL: That's ridiculous! It must have been an atmospheric disturbance.

DAN [*shaking his head*]: No, the compass has become highly magnetized. Don't touch it.

[AUDREY *points right.*]

AUDREY: Look! The shoreline is gone. I can't see the lights anymore.

[*Everyone looks right.*]

DAN: There's a heavy fog on the coast, that's all, and we can't see

151

through it.

BILL: There wasn't any fog a few minutes ago.

DAN: But the *Marie North* signaled about the fog. It must have swept in from the ocean.

MAYBERRY [*sharply*]: Glover! What's wrong with the generator? We're losing power!

GLOVER: I'll go check it out. [GLOVER *dashes down ladder, exits up right.*]

TURNER: Sir, I can't reach Miami anymore. There's something wrong with the radio and the radar equipment.

MAYBERRY: It must be the generator. [*He glances at compass.*] The compass needle is still spinning. [MAYBERRY *stares straight ahead.*] I don't know the direction. We're driving and I don't know where.

AUDREY [*excited*]: I see something in the distance.

DAN [*squinting*]: I can't see anything.

BILL [*looking*]: I think it's a fog bank. A great wave of mist. [*Suddenly*] Audrey's right. Something is moving beyond that fog.

JANE: Yes, I see it too. It looks like a large ship. [*Frightened*] It seems to be bearing down on us.

BILL [*urgently*]: Captain, the vessel is moving to starboard. [MAYBERRY *swings wheel sharply to left.*]

MAYBERRY: Turner, what's happening with the radar?

TURNER: Still dead, Captain. [*Adjusts headphones.*]

BILL: The ship is still headed in our direction.

DAN: It's much closer now. [*He gasps.*] I think it's a freighter. A large freighter.

[AUDREY *descends ladder, rushes to right railing.*]

MAYBERRY: Stop her.

DAN: Come back, Audrey. Don't be a fool! [DAN *descends quickly, pulls* AUDREY *back.*]

BILL [*suddenly*]: I'd better get the life raft and jackets ready. [*He descends, rushes off up right.* AUDREY *struggles with* DAN.]

AUDREY [*frantically*]: Let me go! That's Jim's ship!

DAN: You know that's impossible. Your husband's ship was lost at sea. You must accept that.

JANE [*descending and crossing to them*]: Let me take you to your cabin, Audrey.

AUDREY: No, I'm staying here. [*She points right.*] I can see the ship clearly now. I can almost touch it. I can read the name on the hull.

[DAN *turns right, shades his eyes.*]

DAN [*in disbelief*]: The *Marie North!*

AUDREY [*screaming*]: Jim! [AUDREY *presses against railing, extends her arms.*] Jim! Jim, please, come back! [JANE *draws* AUDREY *away from railing.*]

JANE: It's gone, Audrey. Vanished into the mist.

DAN [*in disbelief*]: It seems as though it passed right through the *Enchantress!* Now there's nothing out there but the fog.

AUDREY [*sobbing*]: Jim's gone. The *Marie North* isn't there.

DAN [*gently*]: It was never there, Audrey. We all got a little hysterical and imagined the whole thing.

AUDREY [*insistently*]: No . . . no. Jim is out there. He wants me to come to him.

[BILL *reenters, looks out.*]

BILL [*puzzled*]: Where's the ship?

JANE: Whatever we saw is gone. Maybe it was only fog.

BILL: That's impossible. We saw it. [DAN *indicates* AUDREY, *and motions* BILL *to silence.*] Yes, I suppose we could have made a mistake.

AUDREY [*slowly*]: I'm tired. I'd like to go to my cabin now.

JANE: May I help you?

AUDREY [*shaking her head*]: I'd rather be alone. [AUDREY *exits left, walking as if in a trance.*]

JANE: This has been a terrible ordeal for her.

DAN: That message from the *Marie North* . . . [*He shrugs.*] It was a mistake, of course.

JANE: Do you really believe that?

DAN: No. I guess not. I know I saw a ship there. Jane, the time tunnel theory . . . do you think we could have seen a ship that disappeared five years ago?

JANE: Look at facts, Dan: Our compass has gone crazy; the generator has broken down for no apparent reason; the radio and radar have failed. These kinds of things have happened before to ships in the Bermuda Triangle. No one has found an explanation for them. [JANE *sighs, walks to rail, turns.*] We have to concern ourselves with much more than crosscurrents and tides, longitude and latitude. We must consider time.

[BILL *and* DAN *join her at rail. They talk in pantomime.*

153

GLOVER *reenters, right, and joins* MAYBERRY *and* TURNER.]

GLOVER: The generators are working now, Captain.

MAYBERRY [*nodding*]: Thank you, Glover. [GLOVER *studies compass.*]

GLOVER: The compass is steady again. It's pointing true North.

MAYBERRY [*nodding*]: Turner, have you been able to reach Miami?

TURNER: No, sir. The radio seems to be O.K., but I can't get a response.

GLOVER: Have there been any other messages from the distressed ship?

TURNER: Nothing. It's like sailing in a vacuum.

MAYBERRY [*to* GLOVER]: The *Marie North* passed our course a few minutes ago.

GLOVER [*in disbelief*]: What?

MAYBERRY [*nodding*]: It appeared at the starboard bow and disappeared into the fog. It was on a direct collision course with us.

GLOVER: I can't believe it. [*As they talk, a series of red lights blink off right, reflected across the deck.* JANE, BILL *and* DAN *look up.* MAYBERRY *and* GLOVER *stand transfixed as lights grow brighter.* TURNER *stands, joins* MAYBERRY *at helm.*]

DAN: What's going on out there, Captain?

MAYBERRY: I've never seen anything like it.

JANE: It's like fireworks.

DAN: But fireworks without any noise. How strange.

BILL: Is it possible that it's an electrical disturbance, like St. Elmo's Fire or the Northern Lights?

JANE: I don't think so. St. Elmo's Fire doesn't act that way. [*She shields her eyes.*] Those lights are blinding. [DAN *ascends ladder.* JANE *and* BILL *follow quickly.*]

TURNER: Captain, the compass is spinning again. [GLOVER *joins him, nods.* MAYBERRY *grips wheel tightly.*]

MAYBERRY: There's that pull again! [GLOVER *glances around.*]

GLOVER: The generators are still working. [*Gradually, offstage red lights fade.* JANE *points upward.*]

JANE: Look at the sky.

DAN [*looking up*]: There seems to be a huge dark shape directly overhead.

BILL: It's trying to land on us! [BILL *throws his arms upward as though to protect his head. He retreats, backs into radio table.*]

JANE: Something's hovering behind that cloud. I think it's trying to reach us.

[TURNER *points up.*]

TURNER: The lights are disappearing behind the cloud, but I can still see them. They seem to be dancing in space!

GLOVER: The cloud is fading. The darkness is melting away. [GLOVER *sighs.*] It's gone. [*He points.*] There's nothing but the stars—and the night. [BILL *rushes forward, tugs at* MAYBERRY'S *sleeve.*]

BILL: What's happening to us?

MAYBERRY [*soberly*]: I've heard of these things before. Glowing lights, a descending dark cloud. This has happened many times in the Bermuda Triangle. Mariners are hesitant to speak about it. They think no one will believe them.

DAN: But this is an important discovery. Perhaps that cloud was an electromagnetic field, something that can literally disintegrate a ship or an aircraft.

MAYBERRY: Who can tell? Navigation is my business, Dan. Not science fiction. [MAYBERRY *grips wheel.*] Right now, I have to get the *Enchantress* and its passengers to port. [*He gestures.*] Turner, get our position. Make every effort to contact Miami.

GLOVER [*looking right*]: There's nothing out there. Not even a trace of light.

[LISA *screams offstage and rushes in. She climbs ladder and throws herself into* BILL'S *arms, sobbing uncontrollably.*]

BILL [*upset*]: Lisa, what is it? [*Urgently*] What is it?

LISA: Dad, it was terrible—terrible!

BILL: Tell me!

LISA: It's Audrey! I saw her disappear!

BILL: What do you mean, you saw her disappear?

LISA [*hysterically*]: I saw her standing on the afterdeck. She looked so strange. Suddenly I saw flashing red lights. They were so bright I had to close my eyes. When I opened them, Audrey was fading into the lights. She became part of them.

DAN: You must have been dreaming, Lisa.

LISA [*sobbing*]: I'm telling you, it happened. I rushed to the afterdeck, but she was gone! Vanished!

GLOVER [*grimly*]: She might have fallen overboard.

LISA: No. She wasn't near the rail. The lights took her away, but she didn't seem to mind. She wanted to go with them. [*She sobs.*] Dad, I'm frightened!

BILL: Honey, don't worry. We'll be in Miami soon.

LISA: We'll never reach Miami. [*She laughs hysterically.*] We'll be another statistic. We'll be lost in the Bermuda Triangle, and they'll never find us. [*Her wild laughter continues.* BILL *shakes her. Gradually, her laughter fades to a whimper.*]

BILL: I'll take you to the cabin. Is Mom still with Aunt Anna?

LISA: Aren't they here? [LISA *glances around wildly.*] They left the cabin to come up on deck.

JANE: We haven't seen them.

BILL: No, they must be below... [*He takes* LISA'S *arm.*] We'll find them. [*They descend the ladder, exit up left.*]

DAN [*in disbelief*]: Audrey can't be gone.

JANE: Those lights and that cloud had a purpose. I think I know what happened to Audrey. [JANE *walks to radio table, turns.*] Everyone on Earth has a counterpart in another system of time. She's gone there.

DAN: Jane, this is insane!

JANE: Do you have a better explanation? And what happened to Meg and Mrs. Bellamy?

DAN: They're in the cabin below.

JANE: I'd like to believe that, but it seems inconceivable that they'd remain below when the generator failed. No, we'll never see them again. They're gone, too.

DAN [*shaking her*]: Will you stop talking like that?

JANE: Every one of us will disappear—one by one!

MAYBERRY [*to* JANE]: I certainly hope you're mistaken!

JANE: Captain, I think the Bermuda Triangle disappearances are due to a parallel world in another universe that has come close to our world, causing people and craft to jump from this world into the other. That could explain the sudden appearance of the *Marie North*.

DAN: But the disappearing passengers—that's crazy.

JANE: Hardly. In the nineteenth century, a French vessel was found afloat with sails set, cargo intact, all hands missing. The *Marie Celeste*.

GLOVER: That's a remote case.

JANE [*insistently*]: The German bark *Freya;* the *John and Mary;* the *Gloria Colite;* the Cuban freighter *Rubicon*—are these remote cases? All of them were found intact, without a single person aboard.

MAYBERRY: Turner, please tell Mr. Armstrong and his family I want to see them at once. [TURNER *exits.*]

JANE [*absently*]: We'll never see them again. We'll never see Turner again. Something is out there waiting for us.

DAN: Stop it, Jane! [*Suddenly, offstage drone of airplane motors is heard. Happily*] Listen! Airplanes! It must be the Coast Guard.

[GLOVER *points right.*]

GLOVER: And the fog is lifting. I can see the shoreline. [*Everyone stares right.*]

JANE: Yes, there is land ahead. But what land? [*Airplane motor sounds increase.*]

DAN [*happily*]: We're heading for Miami! We're safe—that's the important thing.

TURNER [*offstage*]: Mr. Armstrong! Mrs. Bellamy! Where are you? The Captain wants—[*His voice trails off, fades.* JANE *nods thoughtfully.*]

JANE: One by one.

DAN [*pointing upward*]: Those planes are real enough. I can see them now. There are five planes in perfect flight formation.

MAYBERRY: And there is a sixth plane bringing up the rear. [MAYBERRY *grips wheel tighter.*] Five of those planes are TBM Avengers.

DAN: Who cares what they are? They're here to rescue us.

GLOVER [*slowly*]: TBM Avengers haven't been used by the Air Force in more than fifty years. They were World War Two bombers.

DAN: What are you talking about?

GLOVER: In 1945 five Avengers took off from Fort Lauderdale on a routine mission, and then they just . . . disappeared.

DAN [*panicky*]: Do you mean those planes overhead are the same ones? [GLOVER *shrugs.* DAN *shakes his head.*] No don't tell me that! Those planes up there are real. Look! [*He points.*] You're all crazy! I won't believe that we're anywhere but in the Atlantic Ocean, about to reach Miami.

[MAYBERRY *looks up.*]

MAYBERRY: The planes are disappearing over the horizon. [*Offstage motors fade, then are silent.*] They're gone now. [DAN *raises his arms, shakes his fists violently.*]

DAN: No, no! We're down here. You can't stop searching. Come back! Come back!

[MAYBERRY *leaves wheel, walks to ladder, beckons to* GLOVER.]

MAYBERRY: Come with me, Glover. We must search for Armstrong and the others.

DAN [*upset*]: You can't leave your post! What will happen to the boat?

MAYBERRY: It's on automatic pilot. My first responsibility is with our missing passengers. [MAYBERRY *and* GLOVER *descend ladder and exit up left.*]

DAN: What got into Mayberry? How can he take all this so calmly?

JANE: Don't question it, Dan. The Captain has accepted the inevitable. He knows the mystery of the Bermuda Triangle. [JANE *descends the ladder and walks to right rail.* DAN *follows.*]

DAN: We're all alone, Jane. Everyone has gone . . .

JANE: And they won't come back.

DAN: I wonder what the explanation is.

JANE: There are some things we'll never know. "There are more things in heaven and earth . . . than are dreamt of in your philosophy."

DAN [*slowly*]: Yes. Shakespeare was right—strange things. [*He points right.*] Look—the sky is bright as day. And there's the shore!

JANE: Daylight. We must have sailed all night.

DAN [*nodding*]: We foundered in the Bermuda Triangle. [*He points again.*] There's land. [DAN *shields his eyes and squints.*] But I don't see any buildings or people. [*He points.*] And there—in the harbor—look!

JANE [*excited*]: Sailing vessels. Freighters, skiffs, two schooners.

DAN: I've never seen such a display. They're all in clear sight. I can even read some of the names on the hulls.

JANE [*reading*]: The *Sea Venture.*

DAN: The *Patriot.*

JANE: The *Rosalie*—The *Atlanta.* Yes, Dan. They're all the ships that have disappeared in the Bermuda Triangle!

DAN: I think we've reached our port-of-call. I'm not frightened any more, Jane. We're in a strange place, but I've never known such a sense of peace.

JANE: We've been in the time tunnel.

DAN: But we're alive. And I think we'll make it. Even in this world—a world beyond time. [DAN *takes* JANE'S *hand. They continue to stare right. Curtain.*]

THE END